When it comes to

RELATIONSHIPS,

You've been an

IDIOT

By **Dr. Matt,**
FAKE DOCTOR

Visit Dr. Matt online!
http://drmatt.me
and facebook.com/askdrmatt

DR. MATT IS THE AUTHOR OF
Just Stop Having Problems, Stupid!

When It Comes To Relationships,
You've Been An Idiot
Third Edition

Published by Matthew Dean
Photography by Alex Rubin
Design by Matt Kump
Edited by Judy Teto and Lydia Gallant

Contents

*For Bridget, Misty, Brienne, Deb, Becky, Alysha,
Jewel, Audrey, Megan, Loranne, Cara, Desi,
and Nadine, my teachers.*

*And for Alex, who once said something brilliant
enough while we were half-naked in a hot tub
that it became the seed for an entire book.*

The Beginning

"Do you think I should get this vibrator?" said Midgie.

Let me back up.

"Let's go into this sex shop."

No, let's go back further, because if we went on from there, you might start to think that this book was just about sex. It's not. And it's definitely not a book about Midgie. Don't get me wrong! Midgie's great, but this book is about you.

I know what you're thinking: "Dr. Matt, I've been reading your blogs and listening to your podcast and reading your popular bathroom reader, *Just Stop Having Problems, Stupid!* over and over, and you're telling me that after I've been hearing so much about you and how great you are, that now we're going to talk about me?"

You're right. That's probably a bad idea to focus solely on you. I'll share some gems about me just to keep it interesting. In fact, let's add some more flavor and also make it about that person you're in a relationship with. Or the person you're going to be in a relationship with. Either that or the person you've been in a relationship with.

Fine, it's a book about relationships. And if we're going to talk about relationships, let's talk about the ones where you've been an idiot, which, let's admit, is most if not all of them. If you've never been an idiot in relationships, then I'd like to make these two points:

You're a liar and I have no tolerance for liars.

I have no further points. I lied.

Right now you're probably thinking, "Wait a minute, Dr. Matt. If you, The Most Famous Fake Doctor Of Our Time™, say everyone has been an idiot in relationships, then doesn't that mean that you've been an idiot in relationships too?"

That's very clever of you. The answer is no.

Several years ago, I moved from Texas to Canada, and I found a whole bunch of people who, in their politeness, didn't have anyone to tell it to them straight. Fortunately, I've been helping people with their problems ever since I learned problem-solving back on the farm. Let me tell you, if a chicken has a broken leg, politeness is not going to heal it any faster. As Pop used to say, you've gotta either tie a stick to that chicken or heat up the barbecue.

Back in Texas, my clients called me Dr. Matt, as a sign of respect, and also because it was on the sign on the door. Well, Canadians are a bit more picky, and a Canadian lawyer advised me to mention that there was no actual "doctorate" from a "university", but that's a stupid distinction. I mean, did anyone ever tell Dr. Seuss such nonsense? No, they just let him unleash his genius, and let the world decide his qualifications for doctoring. In the same way, telling people what's what is my "O Cat in the Hat, Eat Your Green Ham and Eggs". So to speak.

Having a university doctorate isn't going to qualify you for anything except the fact that you're a good university student. What I am is a life student, and therefore my doctorate is the "doctorate of life". And I've put this doctorate to good use, telling thousands, if not millions, if not billions of people how to live their lives.

Obviously, if I'm advising people on their relationships, then I'm much more likely to have perspective on the whole thing, so your suggestion that I've ever been an idiot in relationships is ridiculous.

However, you've been an idiot, and it's time to just **stop**! Cut it right the heck out!

What's that? You don't know how to stop being an idiot, or even what the heck you've been doing that's idiotic? Well, that's why you bought this book. And if you haven't bought this book and have just picked it up and started reading it in the store like a jackass, then for the love of God, put some money in that shopkeeper's hand so that we can get to it.

(As a note: if you are reading your lover's copy at home in bed, then I'll be talking about you very soon in this book.)

Ready to stop being an idiot in your relationships? Well, okay then.

Just What The Heck Do I Mean By Relationships?

I suppose in order to talk about relationships I should define what kind of relationships I'm talking about. I hate defining things, but my editor says that you'll be confused otherwise, and apparently she knows everything. No, really, she's top notch.

Now, a typical author might say, "Well, gee, I'm not sure how to define this, so let's give you the dictionary definition of 'relationship' first." However, I'm not typical, which my friend the Dalai Lama used to tell me on a regular basis. And I would say that relationships are not defined by terms and example sentences; they're defined by people. And if you think you know what a relationship definitely is, you're wrong.

I know, you're saying to yourself, "Dr. Matt, how is it idiotic if I know what a relationship is?"

Well, I'll tell you why it's idiotic. Because the other person you're in a relationship with also thinks they know what a relationship is, and what both of you don't know is that you don't actually agree. How do I know this? Because depending on who you are, some of you read the word "relationship" and attached words like "romantic", "intimate", "committed", and so on. Some of you also may have assumed that the idiocy I would point out around relationships would likely be highly related to male/female dynamics, thereby attaching the word "heterosexual" to "relationship". But did I say any of that?

To be fair, I'll probably mostly talk about relationships of an intimate or romantic nature, but the dynamics between people tend to be similar no matter what type of relationship it is. Like everything I say, my thoughts on relationships should be applicable to many parts of your life. Because my wisdom is so vast, like the sea or the ocean, you can take segments of these lessons to apply to friendships or even other types of partnerships.

And yes, I'm including the gays. Homosexuals and bisexuals are idiots in relationships too, as are the polyamorous, the kinksters, the celibate, the chaste, and Republicans.

You see, "relationship" covers a lot, so chances are, every nook and cranny that it covers for you is not going to be the same that it covers for anyone else. That's right, you've likely been in relation-ships with a whole mess of people who don't entirely agree on just what it is that's going on between you, and only once in a great while are they actually vocal about the fact that they don't agree. And this usually comes when you're both far from a place where you could agree about things like definitions.

But, if I'm writing to you about relationships, then I guess I need to give you *some* definition to work with. After all, we have to start somewhere. Let's start with this: A "relationship" is the word we use to describe what is created between two people. There, I defined it. What is the thing that is created? Well, exactly, it's different every time. It's the product of those two people.

What do you mean you don't understand? Okay, imagine you are some kind of chemical compound, and so am I. When we meet, we produce a chemical reaction that creates something that is the product of both of us, and may share properties of each of us, yet will also have its own unique properties specific to that relationship. In other words, the relationship is a third chemical compound that is produced from this reaction.

Look, I hate metaphors, and I don't exactly like chemistry, so I'm not happy with this description any more than you are. But it becomes useful to begin to think of the relationship as something that lives separate from the two people who created it. It would not come into existence without them, but it does not belong to either person. Quite the paradox, isn't it?

Midgie is always saying that I like to give people paradoxes. I say I just give people the truth, and the fact that some truths are paradoxical is none of my business. But of course, as a sex educator, her advice tends to be more straightforward. The mechanics of sex, after all, don't change all that much, although, trust me, I don't think Midgie has exhausted all of the possible mechanics. But, as mechanically simple as sex is, there's hardly an area that can get more complicated, and I'll get to that soon.

Another way of describing this other thing that you create in relationships is that you can do things which serve you, which serve the other person, or which serve the relationship. You can have actions which damage you, or your partner, or the relationship. The relationship isn't necessarily damaged when your significant other is feeling hurt, and similarly, the relationship can dissolve even while both people continue on harmoniously.

You could think of a relationship as a type of

house you live in, or the train you're both riding in, or the tandem bike you're both riding. Whatever idiotic metaphor you use, I want you to see the relationship as something that is its own whole separate thing, not a heart necklace that you each have half of.

Why am I insisting that you see the relationship as its own entity separate from the two other entities that have created it? Because when you instead see the relationship as something that you have half of, then you tend to attach the qualities of the relationship as qualities of the people. You attach events in the relationship as causes of either one individual or the other. If it's a bad relationship, you see the other person as bad. The truth is that two good people can produce a bad relationship.

Now you're saying, "Dr. Matt, how is that possible? If the relationship is the product of two people, how can two good people produce a bad relationship?" Well, let's go back to our dumb chemical reaction metaphor. Sometimes the third chemical compound (the relationship), is formed out of the components that are the most reactive. You may have trace amounts of some explosive material, and so does she, and suddenly you get an explosion that destroys anything else that was created. Is the explosion anyone's fault? Does it make one or both of you wrong? Or are you starting to get that there are just some chemicals that should not be mixed?

Even more importantly, two smart people can create an incredibly idiotic relationship, and that's exactly what we're going to be talking about. Or, rather, that's what I'm going to talk about, and you're going to sit there and read it. Why? Well, you want to stop being an idiot, don't you? Then stop giving me so much lip.

Dr. Matt, I'm Still Confused

Right now you're saying, "Dr. Matt, I'm still confused." See? It's even the title of this chapter.

Yes, I know you're confused, and that's exactly where I wanted you. You see, when you picked up this book, you had all sorts of ideas already about relationships. It's the same pile of stuff you take into each and every relationship, and you take it in even if that pile of crap didn't work in the previous one.

So first, we need to get rid of your bag of what you think you know. Men are a certain way, women are a certain way, relationships start like this, relationships end like that, blah blah blah. Look, you can pick up that bag of crap when you finish the book, but first, toss it into the corner. Hey, if you don't, then nothing I say is going to be worth a hill of beans. You'll hear what you want to, and it'll just reinforce that crap bag.

I read once something about men being from Mars and women being from Venus. That's absolute cow dung because I have it on good authority that both environments have atmospheres poisonous to humans. So what's the point of making that claim? Let's get rid of that too.

You don't understand relationships. You don't. You think you do, because you've been told you do. You've been told what to expect, how things go, but strangely, it doesn't quite go that way, does it?

"Wait, Dr. Matt," you're saying. "*That's* not why my failed relationships didn't go the way I expected. It's because the other person was an asshole." Well, my friend, what if you're wrong? Furthermore, what if they would say the same thing about you? Oh, that just proves that they're an asshole? That's kind of circular logic, don't you think?

Maybe you don't think that they're an asshole. Maybe you think that it was as simple as they broke your trust. Sure, I'm not saying people are not responsible for their actions. I mean, if people act stupid, call it what it is. But people are too easily convinced that it's the other person's fault, and that's what's stupid.

Also, note that when I said relationships don't go the way you expect, you jumped on the idea that I meant for the worse. A little touchy, aren't we? Is it possible that you got defensive when I told you that you didn't understand relationships? If you're that attached to what you think you know about relationships, then you gotta know it's a problem.

Okay, I'll back off for a moment. You go ahead and write the things that are universal to all relationships. Here's some space.

Did you write anything? If you did, what did you write? That all relationships involve humans? Sure, I guess we're talking about human relationships, but I don't see how that's useful. Anything else? That all relationships are between two people? Aren't you excluding polygamists? All *healthy* relationships involve two people? Well, you've jumped straight to being judgmental, haven't you? Face it, for anything you might write, there are likely some exceptions.

Now, you'd think with that much variation, that much unknown, and that much diversity in just what exactly goes into a relationship, that any two (or three) people coming together would sit down and discuss just what exactly they think of as a relationship before starting anywhere in that direction. Did you do that? Actually, some people do, but I guarantee that no potential relationship partners can remember to cover *everything*, because life is far too complex. Some people have a conversation like that in the "getting to know you" phase in the relationship, and then forget all about it.

Even if you covered everything, absolutely everything, you still wouldn't have covered everything, because the next day you'd be different, and so would that other person in the relationship.

Now, hopefully, you're getting the picture. Trying to figure out everything in order to have a perfect relationship is a stupid endeavor. Relationships are like a junior high school dance: often awkward, hesitant, and filled with sexual tension. You can't figure out all your dance moves in advance, because you don't know what that other person is going to do. The best you can do is take it one step at a time.

That's what we're doing here folks, just trying to see if we can avoid stepping on that other person's foot, or, with enough confidence, dancing your heart out and letting the other person do the same, hopefully without getting an unwanted erection.

We're emptying out that bag you came here with. You started confused, and that's a good thing. Now you're ready for something new. It's much like the beginning of a relationship. Perhaps you and I are in a relationship, except it's one in which you are not allowed to touch me. These few steps might be awkward, but you've asked me out on a date, a date of knowledge, and that's what you're going to get. All you need to do is open up your brain. And then pay for my dinner.

Dating

When Midgie and I started dating, I thought she was the cat's pajamas. She was smart, funny, sexy, and she had a thing for men with mustaches. That's a pretty winning combination. But she had a lot of gentlemen suitors, so how did I win her over, at least part of the time?

Well, let's think of the idiotic things that *most* people do, which I successfully avoided. Most people put forward an ideal version of themselves, thinking that it's best to hide their faults until they've successfully snared the person, and then they can let some of the cats out of the bag.

That's stupid, and it would have been especially stupid for me to do that. After all, I'm Dr. Matt, The Most Famous Fake Doctor Of Our Time™. So, I just laid down all my faults in front of Midgie. It took me nearly five minutes, but I'm glad that I did it.

You see, we're often concerned with creating and displaying an idealized version of ourselves in order to attract a mate. But, in doing so, we set ourselves up for failure, because on a long enough time-line, we will be whoever we are, not our ideal fantasy about ourselves. We do this because we don't love ourselves for who we are, so we think that it's unlikely that someone else who truly sees us will do the same. We hide behind our delusional fantasy, sometimes projecting forward what we hope to become, who we think we'll be, or maybe just who we think we are on our best days. Folks, this is a waste of energy. And if you've read my last book, and I fully expect that you have, you know that I believe in the importance of energy efficiency. If you expend energy to create a fantasy, and enter into a relationship that way, then you will also expend energy to maintain it. It's like there's a version of Keanu Reeves's Matrix contained within your head, and you're a robot who doesn't have access to solar power so you have to continually plug more energy into your Matrix by converting human body electromagnetism.

Okay, you're right, that part of the movie didn't make sense to me, either. Wouldn't geo-thermal, wind, and wave energy be more abundant and maintainable than siphoning off energy from humans? But that's just it; you're being extremely energy inefficient. The Matrix you've created is dumb. And it's dumb that meddling people can interface with your Matrix without being instantly detected and ejected. I mean, my MacBook knows as soon as I plug my printer in it, and what kind of printer it is, and even how much ink it has left. But someone can enter your Matrix, and you haven't the faintest idea who or where they are, and you only have three robot cops patrolling a Matrix that has six billion entities?

Instead of creating a whole new Matrix (where everyone has designer clothing and knows kung fu) before going on that first date, first make peace with the humans. Obviously, the most important human to make peace with is you.

That's the thing, isn't it? You see, dating isn't about finding that other person. It's about finding who you are. If you think that you're going on multiple dates with someone in order to just find out about *them*, then you're being an idiot. The reason to go on dates is to find out about you, to see what you like: what kind of company you enjoy, what kind of person you find attractive. It's to find out what *you* have to offer, not what they do. That person that you're pursuing is just going to be a reflection about what you want in your life, so it's about you. Some men have a hard time moving out of their comfort zone, so they are attracted to "straws that stir the drink", to women who are adventurous and spontaneous. Some women have a hard time staying in one moment, always thinking about the past and future, so they are attracted to men who are grounded in the world. It's not a gender thing, as those roles could switch, or could happen in equal measure with same-sex couples. And it's not wrong to seek and pursue a relationship with others who offer what you want more of in your life. That's probably why they showed up in the first place. Or it may be because you looked really sexy at that charity event. Whatever the reason, there's no right or wrong about whom we are attracted to, because it isn't about them at all.

It reminds me of a story about my friend Jim, another Yankee import from Tennessee who turned Canadian in the mid '90s. Some time ago, we were sitting at a Japanese restaurant, and Jim had been telling me about his latest relationship. Now, Jim had only dated guys in the past, in a gay way, and so many of his friends assumed that means he was only attracted to men. But this latest relationship started with a female friend of his, and hence Jim's dilemma.

You see, for a long time Jim was fine with calling himself "gay" and built an identity around being a gay man. He also had generally somewhat open relationships, which I don't know what that means, but I assume it means a lot of things that I don't need to picture. Anyway, Jim was worried that he was betraying his identity, and to some degree, she was worried about it too. On that day at the restaurant, Jim explained the ordeal.

"She asked me, would I need a man at some point?" he said.

"Well, would you?" I asked him. The server brought some Japanese spinach salad, and I dove right into that stuff, 'cause boy howdy was I hungry.

Jim replied: "I don't know. I'm ready to try something new, and I feel like it'll be fine. But... what if I'm wrong? What if I do need that?"

I shook my head as the rest of our food arrived. "Jim," I said, "your problem is that you think sexual identity is who you are."

Jim frowned. "What do you mean, Dr. Matt? If it's not who I am, then what is it?"

I paused while I took a bite of a piece of salmon sashimi, which was absolutely delicious. I continued: "Sexual identity, Jim, is what we form to explain how we've felt, what our experiences have been. These identities are mostly about the past. Sure, we can use them to inform the future, but who we are now could be something different. For example," I said, "have you ever been this attracted to a woman before?"

He shook his head. "I've been attracted, but not to this degree. This is completely new."

"Exactly," I said, adding some more wasabi to my already spicy soy mixture. "You took on an identity of being gay because up until now, that fairly accurately described your feelings and your experiences. And that's fine. It doesn't make it not true. It's just not who you are; it's who you've *been*. And not only that, it's only a small part of who you've been; that is, your sexual preferences."

I picked up another piece of salmon sashimi. "Look at this," I told Jim. "I used to avoid sushi at all costs. It was really not my preference in food." I took a bite, savoring the taste of uncooked fish flesh. "And now I love it. Does that mean I've betrayed myself? Does that mean that if I spent most of my life disliking sushi, that my relationship with sushi now is doomed? No, Jim, I've changed, and so have you."

"Uh, I think sexual preference is a little different from food preference, Dr. Matt," argued Jim. "I had to grow up fighting to even recognize that being gay was okay. Gays still get persecuted, even if it's diminished over time, and even if it's a hell of a lot less in Vancouver. So, you survive by making friends who can support you, and a lot of that support has been because they've been through the same things."

"C'mon Jim," I said. "I hate to state clichés, but if your friends didn't support you continuing to discover yourself, then they are preventing you from being a rolling stone that gathers no moss."

"Excuse me?" said Jim.

"That may not be the exact cliché, but I'm sure it still works. People who don't keep moving sometimes grow a layer of moss, and then all they see is moss. They see someone like you as threatening, because you've actually got the stones to move forward, and they don't. My suspicion, though, is that your fear of persecution has less to do with your current friends than the memory of what a discovery like this did in your past. You're at another stage of defining your sexuality, or maybe finally un-defining it."

Jim nodded. "It's true, I don't even know what to call myself now," he said. "I don't think I'm bi, because it's not like a 50/50 split for me."

I shrugged, and poked at the yam tempura, checking it for hotness. "Call yourself Jim, for starters. You're a person who can make whatever decisions he likes, whatever choices feel right. Do you love this woman?"

"Yes," said Jim. "Very much."

"Do you think the two of you can have a loving and rewarding relationship?"

"Yeah," he said, "I think we really can."

"That's all there is, Jim," I said, taking a big bite of some crunchy, deep-fried yam in tempura batter. "We have these relationships to enrich each other's lives, to learn things we might not otherwise learn. Sexual identities don't provide you with a magic formula for which relationships will teach you the most. They can sometimes help point you in the right direction, but, ultimately, you make the choice, not your identity."

Jim and I talked a bit more, and he seemed to relax over the course of dinner. From that time, Jim has been in a happy, non-gay relationship, and by following his attraction, has learned things about himself that he never knew. It doesn't mean something "switched" for him, or that he's no longer attracted to men. For that matter, he readily admitted before his non-gay adventure that he was often attracted to women. But he realized that relationships were there to teach us about ourselves. The idiotic thing to do would be to pick relationships based only on what we already knew. Attraction is only the first clue, a tap on the shoulder about a direction in which there might be a potential connection. We don't have to follow those taps. Sometimes it's good just to recognize whatever the tap is showing us and move on.

The *really* idiotic thing to do would be to pretend that a certain attraction didn't exist. Back when the new Battlestar Galactica was on, and Cylon robots were all the rage, a married woman wrote this to my nationally syndicated "Ask Dr. Matt" column:

Dear Dr. Matt,

I'm married, and a girlfriend of mine asked me one day what I did when my husband gets attracted to other women. I told her that it was impossible, that we're happily married, and people who are happily married don't get attracted to other people. The thing is, when I said this, she looked at me like I was crazy. I love my husband and I know he loves me. But she always has good things to say, so I'm wondering, Dr. Matt, am I crazy to believe I can trust him?
-Happily Married in Toledo

This was my response:

Well, HAMIT, as I'll call you now, let me put your mind at ease to tell you that you are not crazy. However, you are—and I say this with the greatest amount of respect—a dummy.

Here's the problem. What you're doing is bundling attraction, love, commitment, and trust into one package and treating them as if they're all the same thing. That's stupid.

Here's what I mean. I'm assuming from this that you and your husband are monogamous. Obviously, if he's lost his ability to be attracted to others, then monogamy is the only possible scenario here. Monogamy is one of many relationship structures that people engage in, one out of many choices that people make when entering into a committed relationship. Monogamy is a choice where both people say, "You're my only sexual partner." A lot of people automatically enter into monogamy when they get married, and a lot of people will say, "Let's open a joint bank account," and "Let's live in the same house." But these are all separate choices. Monogamy is not an automatic consequence of marriage, and opening a joint savings account is not an automatic consequence of monogamy. Each one is a choice, no matter how little it's discussed. Many married people are not mono-gamous; many people who are committed to each other and trust each other go out on dates with other people. And, on the flip side, many people who are monogamous do not have joint savings accounts. Incidentally, when I'm talk-ing about non-monogamy, I'm not talking about individuals who are non-monogamous but don't tell their partner they are non-mono-gamous, because while that is a choice, it is a stupid one, and those are stupid people.

Monogamy is a choice of relationship structure. It's an arbitrary agreement about what each partner will do, but it ain't an agree-ment on what each person will feel. In fact, you could say that monogamy exists so that people will make choices to bond only to each other in spite of what they may feel. Mono-gamy is kind of like a relationship diet, and is a choice like any other diet. Some people stick to a strict diet, which is often a safe option, considering how much crappy food there is out there. Some people take larger risks, and sample a wider variety of food, and even have a piece of key lime pie from time to time. And, don't get me wrong, the occasional key lime pie may contain arsenic. These are all choices of risk that we make.

Attraction, on the other hand, is a biolo-gical response. We will respond favorably to a beautiful sunset regardless of whether or not we declared our love to the moon the night before. We will fall in love with a touching film, and declare it one of our favorites; and doing so does not eliminate our love for all previous films that happened to be made by the Walt Disney Company. Attraction is simply an evolutionary beeper that goes off and says, "Hey, look! Suitable mate! Suitable mate!" It doesn't matter if you're not interested in mating or if you already have a suitable mate, the beeper just goes off whenever it darn well pleases. And it should, it's what keeps the human race in existence. It continues to go off so that if our mate is killed by a mastodon, we can look at the numbers on our beeper and figure out a different way to pass on our DNA.

Your question, HAMIT, was basically, "The qualities that allowed a relationship with my husband to occur; that is, that he was able to feel love for another, to be attracted, and to bond with another human being, despite his previous attachments in this way, I believe all those qualities have now been eliminated entirely, and he exists as a kind of Cylon pseudo-human who can only emulate these qualities with respect to me. Am I crazy to believe that's true?"

I think the real reason this question is

being posed, this quest to have a Cylon husband, is due to the fear that if you allow yourself to acknowledge that yes, he is still quite human and is attracted to other people, then you must acknowledge that it's possible, entirely possible that he may bond with another person in the same way that he has bonded with you. It's the terrifying fact that when it comes to relationships, we are not in control, despite that ring on your finger, despite that certificate with a number of signatures on it, despite those words you said to each other, despite how much the two of you love each other in this moment. The future is, for all of us, unknown. I mean, look, the Walt Disney Company might make another movie, and I may decide that Monsters, Inc. is no longer the animated movie I look upon most fondly. I highly doubt it, but yet I must acknowledge the possibility.

I don't say that to scare you further. If anything, I think that acknowledging that the man you married is still human is a way to make your choices count for something. Otherwise, you're in a monogamous relationship with someone who doesn't exist, and imaginary relationships never seem to end well.

Having said that, since I'm urging you to accept some possibilities outside your comfort zone, I think it's only fair that I accept the possibility that your husband is a Cylon, and is able to reprogram himself at will, until such point when he joins the other Cylons in a conquest of the human race. If that were true, then yes, it's possible he is attracted to no one but you, but as a side note, marriages to artificial life-forms are not considered valid under the law. But, as a side side note, if Republicans in the U.S. are in power in the future, then it's entirely possible that the ability to marry a robot will be made law before gay marriage is, which will be justified by Republicans who will say that robots are only a threat to our lives and not to the institution of marriage… as long as the robots are not gay. Because there's nothing a Republican fears more on this earth than a gay robot. How can you make that robot feel shame about his gayness? You simply can't.

-Dr. Matt

This response got some criticism, I think mostly by those in the field of robotics, but the points are all still valid.

Attraction gets us in the door, when it comes to dating, and pretty soon our rational brains step in to try to figure it all out. Because, while dating is about figuring out what it is that you want, it doesn't mean that who that other person is is irrelevant. But it does mean that it may be less important than you've ever considered. Even if you think you've discarded all the clichés about dating, many of you still believe in some type of perfect alignment of another person with yourselves. For some, you think of it in spiritual, internal terms, using terms like "soul mate." Others of you externalize that alignment, thinking that the other person needs to overlap with you as much as possible in terms of what they do or how they spend their free time.

Let me just put both notions to rest. If you were to find someone who was 100% in perfect alignment with who you are as a person, then *why the heck would you even need a relationship with them?* What exactly do you think that relationship is going to teach you? What exactly do you think you're going to gain? Sure, maybe it's useful to see yourself in another body, to get a third-person perspective, but you could keep a journal and read it for the same effect. Or you could invent an online persona of yourself as another character. I hear that people do that.

The main problem with this goal is that it is ultimately immature and unrealistic, and borders on fantasy, if not full-on plays in it like a monkey in a sandbox. There's no such thing as a perfect person for you, or someone who perfectly aligns with all of your goals. A friend of Midgie's was very passionate about tennis. She started a relationship once convinced that it would succeed based almost entirely on the fact that they both loved tennis, plus that they had other active activities that they both loved doing. One day, her partner injured his arm, and suddenly the amount of overlap in their activities greatly diminished. Since this was a major component for the relationship, the relationship suffered and ultimately ended. Later, she dated a guy who only seemed mildly interested in tennis and other activities that she liked doing, although he was passionate about different things in his own life. For her, it wasn't enough; she wanted a partner to share everything she did, and she stepped out of the relationship. That second guy went on to become tennis legend Andre Agassi.

Okay, that last part isn't true, but I like stories that end that way. The point is that by seeking perfect alignment for the sake of alignment, you overlook some fundamental problems:

1. *that alignment is impermanent, as much as it supposedly exists,*

2. *it doesn't consider the reality of people as constantly changing, and*

3. *it sets up unrealistic expectations on both yourself and that other person.*

Finally, because you are looking for one other person to fulfill all your needs, or as many as possible, it's a perfect set-up for co-dependency.

Now, after hearing this, you might be thinking that I'm suggesting that you would most benefit by seeking someone as dissimilar from you as possible. But really, that's more idiotic than the first idea. You do need some common ground, just not all common ground. Most successful relationships stem from:

a) *how well you communicate with each other,*
b) *how you deal with and resolve conflict, and*
c) *how good the two of you are in bed. (I'll talk about this one in a bit.)*

In other words, you need a solid framework for discovering and dealing with your differences, not a "perfect" situation where differences are only remotely likely to even arise. Adventure comes from getting out of your comfort zone, and relationships where there is no conflict and you are never uncomfortable are just plum boring.

Maybe I'm getting a little too far ahead of myself. I started talking about the formula for successful relationships, when we had just started talking about dating. It's possible you're only at the casual dating stage. Maybe you haven't even gotten to Date #1, that is, either the first date of your relation-ship journey, or the first date after the end of a com-mitted relationship.

People sometimes ask me, "Dr. Matt, how exactly do I get started? How do I meet people? How do I ask people out?" What I notice is that people often know a lot more about the answers to these questions than they're willing to admit to themselves. What they're really asking is, "Dr. Matt, how do I get over my fears of being visible? How do I see myself as having enough value so that someone else will see it? How do I form the con-nections I want in my life?"

Well, when you read the *real* questions, then I think you start to get a sense of the real answer. Just like Midgie's friend who tried (unsuccessfully) to externally design the perfect relationship, you can't engineer the perfect scenario that will lead someone to you. It's not about finding the perfect person to date; it's about *being* the perfect person to date. This is not to say it's about being perfect, but in dating terms it's about creating a kind of intrigue around yourself. Don't worry about finding those other people; it consumes way too much energy. Let them find you. Let me repeat that. *Let* them find you. That does still mean that you have to be findable.

Hiding in your bedroom is not going to easily lead someone to discover how great you are. Go out, but don't go out for the purpose of meeting that perfect person. Go out for the purpose of being yourself, which is all the perfection that is ever needed. In my case, it's more than the perfection that is needed, but I like to cover my bases.

I was doing a book signing for my book *Just Stop Having Problems, Stupid!* when I met Midgie. She was there with one of her lovers, who has since moved on from their relationship, and lives in Alaska as an aspiring artist. I didn't have to seek her out; I was just there being who I am, and doing what I love to do, and Midgie could see enough to be interested in more. Now, granted, those first few steps took a little finessing and charm, especially since Midgie thought that she had enough lovers the way that it was, but I think I was able to prove that I was plenty worthwhile to add to the mix.

My confidence in that moment was in full swing, having fully recovered after an incident with my good friend Kate that we probably don't need to talk about. It was all just about me loving being Dr. Matt. I don't even know why I mentioned Kate, as it's completely not relevant.

So, anyway, this is key: the more you have a sense of Self, and love that Self, then the more beautiful and sexy and attractive you will become. Yes, there is the practical side of it. The most beautiful painting in the world isn't going to affect people's hearts if it's stuffed away in a private collection. First, recognize that beauty. Second, take that painting that is you and put on an art show.

What I'm talking about, of course, is confidence. One of the best examples of someone lacking confidence was a man who came into my apartment/office about two years ago. I'll call him Ed, or better yet, a fake name like Freddle. I'd better add a last name so that would be something like McMannohaggonbaum. And if you wanted to pry and we needed a middle name, we could just use Dolly-Parton. So, just so we don't get lost, that day I was paid a visit by Freddle Dolly-Parton McMannohaggonbaum.

Anyway, Freddle said to me, "Dr. Matt, how do I become a more confident person?"

I thought to myself, "Well, maybe you could stop being such a pathetic loser," but I didn't want to sound too harsh, so instead I said to Freddle, "Do you think that perhaps you're being too much of a pathetic loser?" (As you can see, by putting it in the form of a question, I greatly reduced the harshness.)

Freddle looked a little stunned, and I figured my

directness surprised him. I continued: "Look, Fred, no one expects you to stop being a pathetic loser overnight. Confidence is–"

"Excuse me, Dr. Matt," Freddle said, interrupting. "But I'm not a pathetic loser."

I said, "Ah ha, but that's how you feel, isn't it? Fred, how can you be a confident person when you don't feel that you are a person deserving of confidence?" Freddle looked confused, but Fred was no dummy. He just couldn't get it right off the bat, because part of his mind kept repeating to him a lie about himself. He had developed a pathetic loser mind, and all that his pathetic loser mind could do was say, "Oh, by the way, I'm a pathetic loser." A pathetic loser mind will literally take you to a party and try to fit into every conversation: "Did you hear? This guy here is a pathetic loser." And then the pathetic loser mind will tell you to eat all the Hint-Of-Lime Tostitos.

I explained to Freddle Dolly-Parton McManno-haggonbaum that we often fool ourselves into thinking that we have to build our confidence, like it's a skill that we have to learn. Well, no, not exactly. Confidence is our natural state of being. Did you hear that, people? Confidence is where we naturally would be, but then things started to get in the way when we were growing up. Enough people said,

"Oh by the way, you're a pathetic loser," that we started to believe them. Little did we know that those people were already pathetic losers and they should have been punched in the face.

For Freddle some of it was more recent. "How can I feel any different?" he said. "My ex-wife used to berate me in front of other people. She seemed to love to emasculate me publicly."

"First of all," I said, "I've met your ex-wife. Is that someone's opinion you really want to value? I mean, when they were handing out crazy-psycho pills at the rave party, I think she stole the whole bowl." Freddle looked ready to defend her (or rather his pathetic loser mind told him to do so), so I quickly said, "Look, I'm not trying to be mean here, but the things you've been told are ridiculous things by even more ridiculous people, people who have no authority to say such things. Your ex-wife had no authority to say any of that stuff, and the thing that's hard for you is to admit that you know that she knew that she had no authority. In fact, the fact that she knew she had no real control over you terrified her, and made her want to do it even more. She was terrified that any minute you would discover what a pathetic loser she was, at least in her own mind."

Freddle seemed to get it, but after a moment, shook his head. "Even if I accept that," he said, "the damage is still done. I still feel like a pathetic loser."

I was starting to understand why this guy was such a tantalizing target to his ex-wife. I mean, when someone is willing to emasculate themselves, it's not a lot of effort to join in. I'm reminded of the movie Fight Club. The main character started "Fight Club" by beating himself up, and that's when every-one else got interested in fighting him and beating him up. I wish I could say more but you do not talk about Fight Club.

"Look, Fred," I said. "I'm gonna level with you here. You have a heap of work to do, but you're not going to get any of it done if you start by telling yourself that it's work that never should have been piled on you. Yeah, you're right. Good for you. You recognize that you never should have had to deal with this work. You're absolutely right that it wasn't your fault, and should not have been your burden. But that doesn't change the fact that the work still exists, and it's still your burden whether you deserved it or not. So if you want to start feeling like a man, start with being willing to do the work at hand. Stop pointing at the construction site and wondering aloud whose fault it is that the concrete is not poured yet. Who cares? You're the foreman; get someone to pour the goddamn concrete."

I was on a roll at this point, and was really

enjoying the sound of my own voice, so I continued.

"Confidence, as I said, Fred, is a natural state of being. You don't need to build it; you need to remove the barriers to it. Bulldoze all that crap. Heck, use some dynamite if you have to and pulverize it into nothingness. Confidence is there like a stuck river, dammed up with the rocks of stupidity. Blow those rocks up with the dynamite of positivity and action." (I believe I got this from Confucius.)

Freddle took a deep breath, and had a little bit of that fire in his eye, because if there's anything a man likes doing, it's blowing stuff up. He thanked me, and, even better, paid me, and left.

This wasn't the last visit from Freddle Dolly-Parton McMannohaggonbaum, and I may get around to mentioning more about that later. But he was a perfect example of what *not* to do, of the effect of a complete lack of confidence.

Whatever you fully embody, confidence or lack of confidence, creates magnetism. Confidence creates magnetic attraction. Lack of confidence creates magnetic repulsion. So you don't have to *do* anything to be attractive. You just need to be fully you, and to know your own attractiveness.

The more you are fully you, the more you can

create the world's most powerful electromagnet. Then, if you want to see perfect alignment, just take a casual stroll through a room full of metal filings.

Flirting

Now, I don't want to give the impression that creating attractive magnetism is the only step, and then you can sit back and just draw people in. You do have to take that stroll where the other attractive bits hang out. You have to fire up that magnet and actually make contact with other human beings. If they're interested, then probably a little ritual will commence that the natives call "flirting."

Flirting is one of the more misunderstood of human activities. Some people forego it because they believe that it has no place outside a committed relationship, or perhaps they feel it has no place in any interaction that isn't for the purpose of pursuing a relationship. And then other people do it constantly, and in the most idiotic way possible. You see, flirting is like advertising. Too much, and you'll look like the outside of a stock car at NASCAR. Too little, and no one's going to frequent your business.

Flirting isn't just like advertising. It is advertising. It advertises what you're interested in, and what qualities in other people you appreciate. Beyond that, it advertises (hopefully) your own best qualities.

Maybe you're uncomfortable with the idea of thinking of flirting as advertising. I mean, it's not like advertisers are the most popular people in the world. Flirting is a way of expressing appreciation, appreciation for that other person and how that person makes you feel. If done right, both people come out of that interaction feeling better about themselves. It's a plus in both columns. If one person flirts like an idiot, then at least one person (although probably both) is going to come out of that experience feeling not so hot.

One of my friends, a professional and attractive woman named Vicky, once raised the question, "But why flirt at all? Why not just compliment a person?" The crux of her question was: why flirt when there's no chance of sexual congress? She felt that it unnecessarily complicated such interactions, especially between friends, and should be reserved for instances of mutual attraction.

Can one unnecessarily complicate interactions? Sure, but people do it without the help of flirting. The thing is, when you make that magnetic connection with someone, sometimes you can add to the level of complication and confusion by *not* flirting. The reason is that, in that moment, when you have that magnetic resonance, flirting is an expression of truth. By distancing yourself from the truth of how someone makes you feel, you can create fantasy or cut yourself off from how you actually feel.

I'm not saying it will never lead to awkward situations, because I've had a doozy of a few. After all, when Midgie started flirting with me, I was confused as all get out, and that girl likes to flirt like bananas like to be covered in peanut butter. I took it as a compliment, but it was an expression of truth that, at the time, seemed outside my sphere of possibility. That is, that she might be interested in an intimate relationship with me, with full knowledge of another man that she was already in a relationship with.

She wasn't sure if it would work. I mean, she quickly saw that I was a boy from a Texas ranch who wasn't used to the many relationship configurations that one might find more common in a place like Vancouver, Canada. That is, if you're only talking about humans. Because, back home, we had three cows that used to like to rastle up a good orgy. Pop used to say that they were energetic enough to be "pre-cooking a steak dinner". So, the concept wasn't a totally foreign concept to me. But just foreign enough that I didn't think that someone might actually make that kind of offer to me.

Flirting was an expression of truth for Midgie, and if I hadn't flirted in return, that would have also communicated a truth. If the idea of a mutual attraction is all in your head, then that truth (that there is no mutual attraction) can allow you to move on. But by my friend Vicky saying that you "know" exactly when to flirt and when not to, I think that grants a level of control and foreknowledge that you don't actually have. It's like finding the "right time" to tell someone the truth. There is no right time but now. (That is, whenever "now" is for you, not whenever I'm writing this. Don't start getting time-spacial on me.)

If Midgie and I had thought that flirting was inappropriate because there was obviously no possibility of a relationship, then the opportunity would have never arrived, because we never would have communicated with each other. Folks, how many times have you talked to old friends, and you both learn that mutual attraction was present but never communicated? It happens to me all the time, because I forget how intensely attractive I am. I'm sure dozens of lovemaking opportunities have passed by because someone neglected to comment on the other person's nice gams.

But, like I said, flirting is not just to find that next lover. Don't be an idiot. Perhaps it's to recognize the gift a previous lover gave to you. Perhaps it's simply to recognize someone's great potential as a lover, period, just maybe not for you. Flirting is just the song that great lovers sing. And if it pleases a listener's ears, so be it.

Of course, at some point, there may indeed be the possibility for more. So, after initial flirtations have commenced, you begin the dance. One person asks another on a date, or perhaps they say, "Hey, I'm going to this party on Saturday night, and you should come." You meet, spend time together, get to know each other, and at some point in the future, if you're both interested in sex, well then someone's pants are coming off. Hopefully, the pants of both parties.

And then, well, it really gets interesting.

Sex

Sex is one area where people probably act the most idiotic. I'm not saying that in the act of sex they do anything particular idiotic (although, let's face it, many do), but certainly people's attitudes and related actions around it are, at best, strange.

Even when dating, when sex is a desired out-come (sometimes a highly-desired outcome), we rarely express how we actually feel about it, or what needs we are seeking to fulfill. Folks, didn't I tell you that pretending at this stage isn't going to get you anywhere?

Hmm, rather than put this in the order of talking about sex in the initial stages of dating first, and then sex in established relationships after that, let's switch that around a bit, because I mostly want to talk about the second part anyway. I know I haven't defined what exactly an "established relationship" is, but let's just say that there are two people who've agreed to spend time together on a regular basis, and they're having sex.

Some of you might be saying: "But Dr. Matt, can't you have a 'relationship' without sex?" Pipe down for a second. Yes, you can; you can have whatever you want. It's just not the type of relationship I'm going to be talking about for the majority of this chapter. So, if you're a nun, and you're reading this to get some insight into your relationship with Jesus Christ, you can skip over this whole chapter if you want to. On the other hand, this may provide you with some much-needed excitement.

Alright, so do we just have the readers left who are interested in sex? And who are interested in or are in a relationship? Okay, then here's the most important statement you will read in this book: HAVE REGULAR, QUALITY SEX.

I'll say that again: HAVE REGULAR, QUALITY SEX. If the first thing to go out the window for you when you are facing something challenging in a relationship is the sex, then it's possible that you don't have the emotional maturity for a long-term relationship. That's right, I did just say that. I'll give you a little experiment. Say you have a fight with your lover. Say, as a result of the fight, the two of you don't feel in the mood for sex. Now, say, instead, that you and your lover decide to open to each other and have sex anyway. If you are both still angry after that, then you missed the second adjective in my statement.

Bonobos, which are a type of ape, do this very behavior. If you offer an unexpected object to two bonobos, they will first establish their cooperation by briefly making sweet bonobo love, and then they will examine the object together. Other apes will squabble and fight about the unexpected object that has altered their shared world.

Of course, male bonobos will sometimes resolve a fight (say over a female) by rubbing their scrotums together, so I'm not saying that one needs to model all behavior from bonobos, but let's get back to this idea of what sex provides.

Say you return from a long trip, and you're not feeling connected with your lover. It's hard to remember even the feelings that have drawn you to them in the past. Because you're feeling disconnected, you feel awkward about having sex. Again, turn to my experiment, and do it anyway, in all its fumbly awkwardness, and dive into that sexual passion as far as you can go. Now, after that, see if you can truly feel as disconnected from your lover.

Folks, sex is the language of sexual relationships. Sex is the mode with which we communicate our intimacy with this type of relationship structure. Sex is not just the fun and games you turn to when you feel aroused because someone piqued your lust. To "allow" sex to happen only when "in the mood" is to be completely passive, to absolve yourself of any responsibility for your own sexual well-being, and to willfully disconnect from that other being in your life.

Hopefully, the last few paragraphs have, at the least, raised a few eyebrows, and perhaps given a few people a case of the crazies. I mean, to suggest that you, an independent and proud human being should engage in sexual intercourse when you feel awkward about it, why how dare I? If you've got a full-on case of the crazies, you might think that Dr. Matt is suggesting that you should feel obligated to have sex, or betray your own feelings. Don't be silly. This isn't about what your lover should expect of you. This is just about where you've been an idiot in your relationships, and where you've been an idiot in your relationships is when you didn't have sex because you were afraid of what your partner thought of you, or afraid that they were mad at you, or because you put the needs of others before yourself, or because you simply didn't recognize what your own needs were. In moments like those, you manifest what you are already leaning towards: feeling disconnected.

I bring this up because I talk to a number of

people in long-term relationships who have stopped having sex, and want to know why. There are a number of reasons, but the one I find the most common is that their brains have gotten in the way. Something threw them off track, and they stopped having sex, and they don't know how to start again. Except they do, because, as I said, the mechanics of sex are exceedingly simple, and you know they've practiced the mechanics. But these brains, with their irrational worry and second-guessing, are short-circuiting the sexual connection, and the irony is that sex is exactly the way to re-establish the circuit. The solution to how to start having sex again is to start having sex again.

Of course, this is not exactly a problem when you're with a woman like Midgie. I mean, regardless of whether or not I feel like having sex, Midgie will usually pounce on me like a saber-tooth tiger on a mastodon. As you know from Fred Flintstone cartoons, it doesn't matter how big the size of that mastodon, or how much it resists, that saber-tooth tiger is going to make sure the mastodon is going down.

I should point out that when I have those times when I'm not necessarily feeling like having sex, it's usually because I've worked myself to the bone writing some brilliant article for a popular magazine, or I'm feeling stressed about something like trying to arrange my public speaking schedule. In other words, I haven't taken the time to re-connect with myself, and if I haven't done that, you can be sure that I'm not connecting with anyone else either. What Midgie is brilliant at is getting me in touch with myself in one fell swoop, usually with something she learned at pole-dancing class.

So, I at least want to be careful that you don't misunderstand not feeling like having sex with having a good reason for that feeling. If you sincerely aren't feeling it, because your partner has betrayed your trust or you don't feel safe with them, then what the heck are you doing there in the first place? I'm not saying go for a quick romp then and hope it all works out.

Sure, you gotta know first what's right with you, and you have to get right with you. But that doesn't mean get yourself perfect before you connect with your partner. I'm saying when you love and trust someone, be willing to be vulnerable with them on a regular basis, even when it's uncomfortable—perhaps *especially* when it's uncomfortable. It's how we deepen intimacy with each other, and deepening intimacy is how we continue to learn from each other. Be vulnerable even when it's a challenge, when it feels emotionally difficult, and those are the moments where you will strengthen your relation-ship.

Now, you may ask, why the heck did I jump to sex before talking about establishing trust and rap-port through verbal communication? The reason is that if we don't talk about sex now, early on, you'd just be thinking about it until I said something about it. I mean, as soon as we got into dating, boom, you knew sex was going to enter the picture soon. Also, it's where we have most, if not all, of our biggest issues. So I figure, if we can get through this chapter together, then it's pretty smooth sailing from here on out.

Already, I've got one of you saying, "Man, the next time I see Dr. Matt, I'm going to give him a piece of my mind." That's alright, I understand. Sometimes, I think we have more hang-ups around sex than we do around relationships themselves, and I intend to shake a few of those loose. I mean, who likes to be called emotionally immature because they don't feel like having sex? I wouldn't. I would think that would piss me right the hell off.

Yet, at the same time, while you're all pissed off at me, your lover is in a relationship with someone who is not connecting. They're facing you, but you're not facing yourself. Yes, they have a choice to stay, and they may indeed leave of their own accord. But you've offered a relationship, and without Regular, Quality sex, you withdraw the connection to what you've offered.

Earlier, I described a relationship as something else two people create. Let's say that the relationship is like a bridge you've built, a suspension bridge between two people. With Regular, Quality sex, you add cables and columns to support your bridge. When sex stops entirely between two lovers, the cables begin snapping.

"Wait wait wait, Dr. Matt," you're saying. "You said that it was possible to have a relationship without sex at all. If that's true, then why would a relationship deteriorate without it?"

You're right. I did say that. The reason is because the reasons to have sex have nothing to do with sex at all. And yet they do.

Let me briefly answer your question, before I explain that entirely confusing statement. I said that a relationship is something created between two people. If we go back to our bridge metaphor, then some relationships use simple arches to support their bridge. It spans a small distance, but it works just fine. In addition, it has the required support that it needs, and if it needs to be reinforced, it is reinforced in an entirely different way.

In other words, the maintenance requirements of a relationship are different depending on the type of relationship being constructed. If it is a sexual relationship, then Regular, Quality sex is the typical maintenance requirement for such a project.

"Hold on," you're saying. "I'm capable of looking up the Internet's wiki-thingy on bridges, as well. Could I not just build a truss bridge, thereby eliminating the need for cables?"

Absolutely, that is theoretically possible. One can build an intimate, connected, and deep relationship without sex. To build such a bridge takes time and energy and patience. I've known people who built a relationship for six months to a year before having sex, but they did eventually connect to each other more deeply through sex, and maintained a sexual relationship thereafter. But, yes, we could argue that the type of bridge they built was one where regular sex was not as essential for the maintenance of the relationship.

I met a lot of those kinds of people through Midgie, who is connected with lots of polyamorous people. If you don't know, polyamory means, literally, "many loves." It basically translates to: you don't make one other person responsible for all of your relationship needs. You take the responsibility for your own sexual and relationship well-being. It doesn't mean that people don't form partnerships; it seems to translate to the idea that those partnerships don't inherently limit choice and free will (even if that limitation is typically self-imposed). At the same time, polyamorous people tend to volunteer information that their partners need to know in order to make informed choices, because there's not an expectation that one other person is responsible for asking the right questions. People (in theory) take care of themselves, and the only expectation is that others do the same. Midgie tells me that polyamory was invented by women, while poly-gamy was invented by men. Even though they both involve multiple lovers, you can probably see that they are worlds apart.

Building an intimate relationship without sex is a different kind of bridge structure, so there are a variety of bridges one can build. My question is: which one fits you? Can you be in a relationship for twelve months without sex, and be fine with that? Could you be fine with your lover having other lov-ers? There's the theory of how relationships can be, and there's the reality of what relationships are for you.

I couldn't really get into that polyamory stuff that Midgie does. It's not a problem of her being with other lovers. She does it in a safe way and, I mean, who's going to stop her anyway? She's a wildcat. No, it was more a time-management issue for me. I've got my hands full with Midgie, at least when she's around, and one more person would keep things from being simple for me. I've got my work, my TV appearances, my book tours, etc. For me, in my life, one is enough. There are things I want to accomplish and, while it might seem fun, multiple lovers would just slow me down.

You didn't forget what I said earlier, did you? I said, "The reasons to have sex have nothing to do with sex at all. And yet they do." Why? Well, because of this, which is the most important statement you will read in this book: SEX IS NOT THAT IMPORTANT.

Sex is a path on the bridge, but it's not the destination. So to treat it like this all-important thing in relationships is just idiotic. It doesn't *really* matter how frequently you're having sex. So, why did I so adamantly say otherwise? Well, because I like stirring the pot. And now it's time to disencomfortize the people who excitedly agreed with me when they thought I was "on their side" and they could say to their partners: "See! Dr. Matt says we should be having sex regularly! And if we don't, you're sabotaging the relationship!" Don't be an idiot. I said nothing of the sort. Furthermore, if you're that person, you're probably reading your lover's copy of this book instead of buying one of your own, so you can guarantee I'm not on your side.

Sex is important in relationships because it is part of the bridge to intimacy, but that doesn't mean that sex is the whole goddamn bridge. You can't just have regular sex and expect it will solve all issues that might arise in the relationship. Arranged marriages probably have lots of regular sex. Of course, I did use the word "quality" as well, which probably wouldn't apply there. But, just the same, even Regular, Quality sex means little without a sense of what it's for. The goal is not sex, just like the goal of sex is not orgasm. If you think that it is, then you have no idea what I mean by "quality," do you? And to your lover: I'm sorry.

In fact, your expectations and attachments to sex may be part of the problem. How can two people build a bridge when you're the only one deciding on all the materials required? Even the person not wanting to have sex can be stuck there for the same reasons: their expectations and attachments to sex, and the idea that it needs to unfold a certain way.

So how should sex unfold? Well, didn't I just say that there wasn't one set way? Let me put it this way. In the practice of Kama Sutra, a lot of the described moves or positions many of us would consider sensual but not necessarily sexual. They are designed for what is important, which is connecting with your lover. Ever done something like yoga or Pilates? If you have, they'll have you do a position first, and then they may describe what part of your body you are strengthening. Therefore, the positions are not done for the sake of the positions themselves or contorting your body in inhuman ways. It's to uniformly build unseen muscles under the surface, even though it can make the Lululemon-wrapped surface look mighty fine.

It's the same in sex. Sex is a physical language which one can build and broaden and explore in multiple tongues. Sure, the sex itself is fun, just like other physical activities can be fun. But it is connecting us with something unseen, something between each other, a connection which goes beyond who we are as individuals.

Just like any physical discipline, it does take time to learn the forms that work, because the forms that two people will create are unique every time. Yes, there are lots of suggestions out in the world for what forms to try, but in my private sessions with lovers, I find that two people will eventually "stumble" upon the "perfect" position. It really isn't a universally perfect position; it's simply a form that resonates a communication of intimacy between the two lovers. In my experience, such discoveries can take months or even years, depending on how open the two lovers are to each other. Sometimes, two lovers will find that resonance of communication very early on, because they both happened to be open in the same way, either by luck or intention or just because they are just two very hot people. Or, like in the case of Midgie and me, both are true.

Since I bring up those two hot people, now seems like a perfect opportunity to talk about those initial sexual experiences. I mean, you're here reading this business about the Kama Sutra, and sex as it relates to bridge-building in relationships, and it could all be somewhat intimidating. What, one sexual experience and suddenly you've erected a bridge that is going to come crashing apart without more sex?

Well, let's say that some forms of sexual interaction are like the instant bridges that special U.S. Army vehicles can quickly construct, and just as quickly collapse. Yes, dear friends, I'm speaking of casual sex. Now, before you gasp and hold onto the edges of your Victorian dress, this is a type of bridge that can be safely built between consenting adults, and subsequently disassembled. However, it's not for everyone. As I've said before, many people have too many attachments to sex for such adventures, and that's okay. For example, Midgie is one of those people who can attach and detach, no problem, but I tend to become quickly attached to my lovers. There's no right or wrong here. It's just a matter of knowing what bridge-building materials you bring to the table. Obviously, there are fools who really can't build and disassemble this type of bridge but think they can anyway, and they end up feeling hurt.

Midgie and I have a friend Gunther who was always fascinated by Midgie's tales of sexual adventures. Eventually, he pressured his girlfriend to participate in activities in which she was not comfortable, which was already pretty stupid. Then, when she ended their relationship, Gunther took this as an opportunity to embrace the wild lifestyle that he heard being described. The only thing was, what he heard and what Midgie was describing were two very different things. His dream of con-sequence-free sex with endlessly willing, emotion-ally-detached, and instantly available women never quite came to pass. Oh, he was once successful in a casual sexual experience at a party with two friendly ladies, but as Midgie told me later, his own fears of inadequacy in this situation came up sud-denly, and he wasn't so accepting of the idea that the two ladies were unwilling to repeat the experience. He discovered, quite jarringly, that he had hang-ups with sex that were incompatible with his fantasies. In the end, you could still say that he had quite a learning experience, so the fact that he was exploring was not so bad. But if you're going to be an idiot in sex, then casual sex is about the most idiotic place to do it. The most obvious poor result is that you're going to erect a bridge that you haven't the faintest idea what to do with, and as I've already stated, there are fewer things more embarrassing than an ill-timed and unwanted erection.

But hang on. We've been talking about only the more challenging aspects of sex, and I wouldn't want you to think that, with all this talk of bridge construction, sex has to suddenly become complicated. In fact, complicating sex is about as idiotic as treating it flippantly. The point isn't to go all up in your brain about it. This is probably the one area in relationships where your body is pretty good at calling the shots, and all you need to do is relax and allow some good times.

What I'm doing is giving you the rules, so that you can learn the rules and then forget about them. Take those who do casual sex well or, heck, *correctly.* They are people who have taken the time to learn effective bridge design, but do you think they're thinking about the exact shape of instabridge while enjoying an evening with their friend with benefits? Even if you have no friends with benefits, the same rules apply. Be smart about your choices, but then, for Pete's sake, *enjoy* the choice you've made. Take that choice out for a test drive and see how fast it can go. Don't worry about your choices. It will reveal itself to be in your best interest or not. After all, if you're going to make a mistake, at least dress up in a cowboy hat and spurs and allow your mistake to be a hell of a good time.

You don't have to worry about every detail about the construction of a bridge, because these bridges will fairly naturally build themselves, based on what you already know subconsciously about bridge-building. It's kind of like how Neo flies in the Matrix after he figures out that he's "The One". When he was trying to be The One, he fell off a building or something. But once he accepts who he is, he just flies without thinking. Therefore, the more you learn about bridge building, the less you have to think about bridge building.

Having said that, I'm not suggesting you do it unconsciously. Even though bridges naturally build themselves, you can alter their construction along the way. After all, if you know anything about bridges (and I hope you do by now), you know that while the concept of their construction is fairly simple (go from here to there), their design and form can be quite different. As you become more conscious of the bridge and its construction, your freedom to modify that bridge and paint it pretty colors will increase.

But remember, folks, that it isn't just a bridge that *you* are building. There are these other beings who are involved in this construction process as well, and all of this construction is happening simultaneously. In fact, that other person that you're with is building all kinds of bridges while they're building one with you. The other bridges may be simpler, especially if they don't involve sex, but it's all going on right now.

Obviously, then, there is an element of free will for that other person. But, just the same, you can positively affect the construction of the bridge between you and another person. Who knows? Maybe you can build a new kind of bridge that never deteriorates, no matter if it has zero future investment from either person. If that's getting a little bit ahead of ourselves, maybe you can at least build a more solid one than you have in the past.

Because the building of your bridge may involve more than one person, you may want to know just what *they* know about bridges, and what they intend to build. That means you gotta open that big yapper of yours and start talking to that other person about drawing up some blueprints.

Communication

Now, as we all know, the most annoying character in the *Matrix* films was a dude who called himself "The Architect." He had apparently constructed this whole matrix, that all the people in the world were connected to and somehow generated batteries for machines. The problem was, as was painstakingly described in the second film in 10,000 minutes of screen time, that he did this construction without consulting the other people involved. Therefore, instead of participating in the Matrix, they decided to learn kung fu and fight robots.

What The Architect and the humans could have done was have a chat about what they wanted to build together. I suppose, though, that since the humans had tried to blot out the sun in order to kill the robots, The Architect being one of them (I think), communication may have been difficult.

Let's assume that you and your partner / lover / boyfriend / girlfriend / whatever are both human, and that one of you is not using the other as an energy source. If so, then you have some common ground to communicate, but let's face it, many of you are poor communicators. Look, just because you think you've mostly mastered the English language (or whatever language this book has been translated into at the time you are reading it), it does not make you a good communicator. Communication is not a matter of language; it's a matter of receptivity.

A lot of people think that they communicate because they talk actively *at* their partner, constantly flapping their jaw like a bonobo in a bathtub full of ice water. Volunteering information *is* important, but I've seen annoying clients who hide behind their communication. They talk and talk as a way to control what is said. Sure, they're volunteering information, but they're volunteering only the information that they want to share, and manage to steer clear of any topic which might be the least bit uncomfortable.

As I proved to you at the beginning of this book, relationships are completely undefined. There is no one perfect model for them. Therefore, communication is not about trying to get your point across; communication is about seeking common understanding.

Oh, I see. There's a reader there, yes right there,

who is nodding like they've heard this before. Yes, you, dear reader, who thinks you know all about listening, which you assume I'm now going to talk about, and I can't possibly say anything new that you haven't heard before.

Alright, fine, I see I'm going to have to dig a little deeper with this one. I'm going to have to say something really outlandish for you to change your perspective for what you think you know about communication.

I love Justin Bieber. I think there's something intriguing about his music, and he has a down-to-earth quality of connecting with his fans.

Okay, that's a pile of cow dung, because I don't think I've ever heard a Justin Bieber song. But now that I've defied your expectations, you're actually listening, instead of sitting there with that smug I-know-what-you're-going-to-say look on your face. Having expectations and preconceived notions for the outcome of future conversations is where people act like morons all the time. It's as stupid as having expectations and preconceived notions about the relationship itself. That other person has had a whole lifetime of experiences that you haven't had, which shape the way they think and how they respond to information. So don't act like you know what they're going to say, or wait until you communicate something because you "know" it will upset them, and exactly in what way they will be upset.

This reminds me of two clients that came to visit me, a newlywed couple named Tom and Julie. Tom and Julie had a problem. You see, Julie had recently decided that she wanted to move to Spain. She came to Tom one day and said, "This is what I want."

This was a bit disturbing for Tom, because, for one, he was not fond of sangria. But in general, it was such a major change from where they were living now that he felt a bit overwhelmed about it. Julie had told him what part of Spain she wanted to live in, the house she wanted, and even what she wanted to do there all at the same time.

I listened to both of them and then turned to Julie. "Julie," I said, "it sounds like you made this decision without really talking to your husband about it, even though it directly affects your relationship."

"What do you mean?" she said. "I presented what I wanted. I told him about it, and we're talking about it here. I was hoping you could help Tom figure out what he wants so he can give a counter-proposal."

"A counter-proposal?" asked Tom. "What does

that mean?" I was pretty curious myself, but I had an idea of what Julie would say next, because I'm pretty good at guessing.

"Well, the way I see it," said Julie, "I give a pro-posal of what I want. Then Tom gives a coun-ter-proposal, and we find our way to the middle."

Now, folks, I don't know if you can see the flaw in this line of thinking, but I could. "Julie," I said, "I'm sorry, but that sounds downright stupid."

"What?" said Julie, shocked. Tom also looked a little surprised, so I was glad to have both of their full attention so that I could knock some wisdom into them.

"A relationship is not a negotiation," I said. "A relationship is a collaboration. Instead of both of you talking about the issues, and talking your way through the process, you've slid an entire package about what you want across the table, a whole life of what you want, to Tom. But from hearing you describe it, it sounds like the contents of the pack-age have been sealed and the origins of the package are unknown. You've wrapped both the issue and the conclusion of how to fix the issue into the same package."

"That's exactly what it feels like," said Tom.

"Tom, just be quiet for a second," I said, wanting him to shut the heck up lest I lost my train of thought. I turned back to Julie. "Sliding an entire package over to Tom sounds like a way to try to control the relationship to me."

"I'm not trying to control the relationship," denied Julie. "I said that I'm completely open to a counter-proposal. How else will we come to an agreement?"

"Well first, you start by throwing away your proposals and counter-proposals," I said. "That's stupid. What you're at least doing is attempting to control the process, which still means that you're not working with Tom from where your ideas on this originally started. Had you done that, then the 'proposal' you would have ended up with would have been one that you designed together. If you rely on proposals and counter-proposals, then often you'll end up with neither of you getting what you want, because if you each work as individuals you might not find a solution that you would if you collaborated. You're not utilizing the greatest tool you have here to find solutions, which is the relationship itself."

Tom looked like he wanted to agree, so I turned to him before he ran his mouth off. "Julie's right about something, Tom. You do need to find what you want. I think your struggle is that you're trying to find a way to give Julie what she wants, and that's not going to work."

"What you both have been idiots about is that you both are facing the same issues. Tom, your life is not working for you in the same way that Julie's is not working for her. But, Julie, by proposing only the solution, you both have ended up debating the solution instead of talking about the issues and finding common ground. You can't see how perfect you two are as collaborators because you're focusing on this fantasy that Julie has."

"It's not a fantasy," said Julie immediately.

"Julie, do you speak Spanish?" I asked.

"No," she said.

"Well, okay then," I said. "My suggestion is that you start at the beginning. Talk to each other about what it is in your life that isn't working and you would like to see change. The crazy thing is that the solution the two of you come up with might in fact end up being Spain, but I think you'll both feel better if you arrive at that conclusion together. But, for now, don't worry about the outcome or the solution. What you need is to open your communication, and the solution will find itself."

Folks, I sat back and took a deep breath, because that was about the most wisdom I had packed into a single client session. Seriously, if I charged people by the tidbits of wisdom, then I should have charged Tom and Julie $5,000 for that session. However, I felt $500 was plenty reasonable.

Just before we ended, something seemed to occur to Tom and he turned to Julie. "Hey," he said, "isn't one of your university professors from Spain?"

That seemed potentially interesting but we were out of time. I sent Tom and Julie on their way, knowing I would probably be seeing them again soon.

As I mentioned before, Midgie and I communicated quite a bit initially about our thoughts and feelings on relationship structures, and our strategies for avoiding any and all pitfalls. But of course, people change and grow, and communicating about your feelings and needs in the relationship is not something you tackle once on those first dates, and then forget about. You can't assume that that other person feels the same way about 100% of the items in their lives just because they haven't made any outward changes about your relationship, at least none that you've observed.

Midgie and I have a formal conversation once a year about whether or not we want to continue in the relationship. We must both be actively on-board to "renew" for another year, and if we don't, then no hard feelings, and we'll each continue on our way.

Come to think of it, the due date for that conversation is actually coming up here fairly soon. That's interesting... I hadn't actually thought much about it. I guess I'll have to talk to Midgie soon about that.

Sometimes you need to make dates for communication like that. Like sex, communication is something that you sometimes need to commit to doing, and get anything out of the way that would prevent that from happening. But don't get the wrong impression. Just because I'm advising to do these things when they're uncomfortable doesn't mean discomfort would or should be the norm. It's just recognizing that discomfort is not necessarily an indicator of whether or not you should be engaging in an activity. Exercise can be uncomfortable, but that doesn't mean that your body is sending you a message that you shouldn't exercise. It means that your body is sending you a message that you are moving beyond your stasis point, to one of growth. I mean, think about it. Muscle building is literally a process of making thousands of small tears in your muscle fibers. As you know, that's an uncomfortable process. But moving through that discomfort leads to growth.

All this talk about muscle building reminds me of one of Midgie's lovers a couple years ago, a friend of mine named Roger. At the time, Midgie and I were not living together, and we were just starting to talk about transitioning our relationship from just exciting lovemaking to something more like a partnership.

Roger and I would work out at the gym together, and we would support each other by spotting one another and complimenting each other on our progress,commenting on how the other person's body was changing and growing. Roger was very environmentally conscious, and he would often suggest that we conserve water by only using one shower. He sometimes suggested that we conserve the soap in much the same way, but that made me a little uncomfortable. Other than that, we had a great relationship.

Since we had Midgie in common, she was often a topic of conversation. One of the things that Roger had a hard time with was Midgie's regular attendance at church services. Roger was very anti-spirtuality, so the fact that Midgie went as far as to sometimes give sermons at her church (which is some kind of new-agey tribute to the Universe or some such) really bothered him.

The thing is, he could never bring himself to talk to Midgie about it, because he was worried that it would offend her. Actually, it's probably more correct to say that Roger, like most atheists, assumed that if he confronted her about how illogical her beliefs were, then Midgie would realize the error of her ways and the shock could shake her world apart. The amusing (and sometimes annoying) part to me is that Roger was a lot more dogmatic and imposing in his beliefs than Midgie ever was. If you ever defined the personality of a religious zealot, Roger fit the bill.

So, while he couldn't bring himself to confront Midgie about it, he would often bring it up with me. One day as I was bulking up my pecs on the chest press machine, Roger mentioned that Midgie was going to be speaking on Sunday. "I want to go listen to her," he said. "She's got a great topic she's talking about, something to do with your body as a temple that believers would enter, but I don't want to go to something that's called 'church'. I have a lot of negative associations with that word. Why do they have to call it church?"

I realized I couldn't ignore Roger's problem any more. Since we were weight-lifting buddies, he had suddenly made it my problem. I dropped the weight on the stack, feeling the bulge of my pectorals through my shirt.

"Roger," I said, "let me stop you while you're ahead. First, your problem is that you want to make your problems into other people's problems. They're not calling this Sunday service or whatever it is 'Ritualistic Human Sacrifice' or 'The Crusades' or 'Holocaust Denial Celebration'. If you have a negative reaction to something that's fairly generic, it's not their job to make it okay for you. You're not obligated to go, so they're not obligated to make it more neutral for you. If church is something you don't want to go to, don't go."

"But I want to listen to Midgie," he said, looking like a downcast five-year-old.

"Then go. Do you have to perform some ritual in order to enter the building?" I said, nearly at my wits end.

"No," said Roger. "I'm sorry, Dr. Matt, I don't know what my hang-up is." We made our way over to the Gravitron machine, which if you don't know, is a machine that balances your mass so that you can easily pull up and down. Recently, I described this device to Midgie, and she had a device built on the same concept in our bedroom.

But, back to our story. As I was spotting Roger, I said, "Roger, why is it that you've never talked to my Midgie about this?"

He shrugged. "I don't want to offend her. I mean, it's not up to me what she does. We don't have the same relationship that she has with you."

I'm not sure what he was trying to say there, but I let it slide.

"Roger," I said, "I'm not suggesting you tell her in order to change her mind, you nincompoop. I'm suggesting you tell her to talk about *your* problem, not hers."

He frowned at me. "What do you mean?"

"You have a problem with her spirituality. Midgie doesn't have a problem with your atheism."

He seemed confused. "Why would she?"

I was about ready to slap this guy in the face. Sometimes it's so irritating how blind zealots are to self-perception.

"Listen," I said, "don't you have a pretty high opinion of Midgie?"

"Of course," said Roger. "She's one of the greatest people I know."

"Absolutely," I said. "She is extremely versatile

in everything she does. And fun."

"Lots of fun," he said.

"Extremely pleasurable to be around," I said.

"There is no one who gives greater pleasure," he said.

"Right," I said. "And she's speaking at this thing called 'church'. But I bet your story of her hasn't changed."

"No, not really," he said.

"Exactly," I said. "People believe a lot of different things, about the nature of their reality, their purpose in life, or if they believe they have purpose at all. But they stay who they are. Your perception of them is not based that much on what they do or what they believe. Or if it is, your story is not likely to be that accurate."

"That's true," he said.

"Here's the real kicker," I said. "What if someone else had dragged you to a church service, and you met my Midgie for the first time? What if you found out she went to church all the time?"

Roger looked at me sheepishly. "I probably wouldn't think much of her," he said.

"Exactly right," I said, "which means that your

judgement on the nature of spiritual people is probably as misguided as your judgement about the nature of the Universe, or its lack of one."

"I don't understand," he said.

I sighed. "The point is, Roger, that it's your issue, and it's an issue that's keeping you at odds with Midgie. You think that what's keeping you at odds is *her* beliefs, but that's a bunch of horse manure. It should be obvious to that rational brain of yours that what's keeping you at odds is your beliefs about her."

Roger went deep into thought after that, and didn't really say much until he made some small talk in the shower.

The unfortunate thing is that Roger couldn't ever get around himself. His arrogant belief that he understood the nature of their relationship, without communicating it, ultimately put him more and more at odds with Midgie. I'm sure he'd still insist that she discontinued their lovemaking because of his atheism, and the facts will never convince him otherwise. This is unfortunately true of most atheists.

Folks, you have to communicate with your partner, and you need to do it because it creates continual growth in your relationship, or at least because it demolishes meaningless barriers. In fact, that's one of the most important times to communic- ate: when there's a barrier to communication, such as when the two of you are at odds. Not sure where to start? Well, Pop used to say that the hardest thing to know is when you're wrong, but luckily there are women around to help you.

And certainly, the point of communication isn't that you have something fantastically interesting to say, or that your partner is the most interesting per- son around at that very moment. I mean, let's con- trast Roger with an earlier lover that Midgie dated for a short while, a jackass named T.J.

T.J. would often say, "That's boring," as soon as someone talked about a topic that he found boring. He argued that he was simply being honest, and why should he pretend to be interested in a topic that he wasn't actually interesting in? Well, the reason is because the topic is irrelevant, and if he wasn't such a jackass he would have seen that. People don't talk to each other about sports scores or fashion or celebrity news because any of that stuff is remotely relevant or important. The reason why people use those topics is because they are a common bridge to connect with one another. I've sometimes been standing in an elevator, and if I'm in that elevator alone with a man, then more often than not, he will make a sports-related comment. He may not be interested in talking about sports in that moment, but it's a just a common technique among men to initiate connections with other men. The conversation isn't important. In fact, because I was never huge on sports, I often found it confounding why men would state sports knowledge that all of the other men in a group seemed to already have. Furthermore, at times, they would repeat the same sports knowledge that had already been established in a previous conversation. The simple reason was that shared knowledge and experiences are a bridge builder.

Folks, this is why you talk with your partner about how their day was, and how your day was, or even call them in the middle of the day and ask them how their day is proceeding. The actual events in their day are rarely likely to be of profound significance, so don't be an idiot and think that if you're not interested in those events that you should not ask the question. The point is to connect with each other. Partners who do not connect every day, either through communication or sex or both can have a hard time maintaining their relationship. Sometimes partners find it hard to connect to each other because one of them travels often, or is out of reach for whatever reason. At the very least, find a way to connect daily to the feeling of that person. That is, if keeping that relationship is important to you. If it's not, then, by all means, don't communicate and don't have sex, and focus only on yourself. You'll find that the relationship will naturally end without you having to do much of anything.

Just like Midgie's douche-bag ex-boyfriend T.J., some people may be turned off with the idea of having to expend any energy at all at maintaining a relationship. Here's another gem Johnny Dickhead used to say: "A relationship should never be work. If you have to work at it, then you probably shouldn't be in a relationship." Of course, I observed that he was perfectly fine with the other person in the relationship working their ass off to resolve issues. I mean, that was their choice, and who was he to stand in the way of their choices?

Anything we build takes work, and because we don't start a relationship as two people who are as intimately connected as they ever are going to be, then there's going to be work involved to build that intimacy. Just because we use the word "work" doesn't mean it has to be unpleasant, or the experience cannot be fun and joyous. But if you think that a relationship does not take work, then you are a lazy asshole, and I should have punched you in the face when I had the impulse at Midgie's birthday party.

Maybe I'm digressing just a little bit. I mean, I set out to just talk about communication. But sometimes you have to get out of your own way, and stop trying to control what you offer into a conversation. If you want to talk about over-working, it's trying to control the outcome of things. Maybe I should write a whole chapter about control. I hadn't really planned on it, but what the heck. If I run out of things to say, it can just be a short chapter.

Control

Let's start by figuring out just where the heck we're at so far. You've been building bridges, and before this book, you've probably been doing a poor job, but as of now you're going to start getting better. I've told you that you could more consciously build those bridges, and if you didn't do this or that then this would happen, or that would happen. I suppose I might have implied that to do more of one thing automatically reduced the likelihood of something else happening. But, I also told you earlier that what was created between two people was something that developed naturally, and of its own accord. I give you true paradoxes like this so that you'll pay attention.

I also said that no one knows what a relationship is, yet I've described exactly how to proceed in them, which is another paradox. So, what the heck, let's give you one more: everyone has a lot to learn about relationships, but the truth is that you're probably the only legitimate teacher.

The Dalai Lama used to throw things like this at me, and I'd tell him that he didn't know a hill of beans about relationships since he'd never been laid. He'd usually laugh at me and try to pull on my mustache, which was irritating and I felt was just a distraction from the issue. I have to say that I took a different approach than him of reflection from a distance. There's nothing like the richness of direct experience to give you clarity on what's what. That's why you're a better teacher for you than someone like the Dalai Lama, even if he is a good friend—or Mohammed or Jesus or the Pope or Ganesh for that matter. But I feel like we're in danger of getting off-topic, and I've already covered a lot of this in my previous book, so go pick up that one instead. (Again, if you're reading someone else's copy of *this* book, then I should let you know that there's something in this book that is essential for your life, and you probably won't catch it until you've read your own copy several times.)

Anyway, hopefully with some of those paradoxes we've reset your brain circuits. We've kicked your old ideas to the curb and have started to give you a new framework on which to build some better ones. But here's the rub: we've been doing all this so that you could let go of controlling what you think you know about your relationship to relationships, but all the while you've been trying to learn something new because you think that relationships are ultimately something that you can control.

I'll give you a moment to go back and re-read that last sentence, because I realize I just blew your mind with the paradox of paradoxes...

You think understanding relationships is the key to controlling them. Oh, I'm sure you wouldn't put it in terms like that. But you do think that knowing everything about them means that you can more tightly control the outcome.

A client of mine, Dean, thought exactly that. His concept was that if he very consciously and deliberately constructed a bridge with his partner, then it would be so solid as to be nearly indestructible. In other words, his notion was that conscious bridge-building afforded him control. He said to me, "Dr. Matt, if you do things right, relationships don't *ever* need to end." While that statement carries some truth, and I'll get to that later, Dean's controlling nature meant was that he was not allowing himself to see any possible outcome for the relationships beyond the variables that he could control. Wouldn't you know it, those variables are few, and my friend Dean was blind-sided when his lady slept with a ski instructor.

Remember in that Matrix movie, when that one bald guy says that the Matrix was built as a form of control? Instead of imprisoning people, however, all the robots did was present a world which could be lived in and accepted as reality. The control was effective because people participated in that control. They made their lives a kind of self-reinforcing control system. That is until they saw women in red dresses or something like that. I wasn't too clear about that part.

Dean was terrified of an outcome that he couldn't control, and so he embraced a reality where he only saw what he wanted to see. And then, metaphorically speaking, he got flushed down into some kind of sewer and swam about until he saw a bright light and a giant claw pulled him up to a ship where he could learn the truth and how to use advanced weaponry. (In this metaphor, I am the Ship of Truth and my marketing assistant is the giant claw.)

Relationships can be a lot simpler than those bizarre movies. We try to make it complex, but it really is simple bridge building, putting in cable after cable in our suspension bridge to connect us together.

But, perhaps, if we didn't put in the cables using our own energy, and since the thing that is created between two people happens naturally, then we might be able to guide that construction process by acting more as a foreman and less like a construction worker. If there's control, it's in the details. If relationships are work, it should not be grunt labor, day in and day out. It should be the kind of work that is satisfying and rewarding, and where you get paid more.

The more control that you apply to a relationship, the less rewards you will glean from it. When I was kid, there was this Play-Doh machine that you could place shape filters on to, and it would make a snake of a certain shape emerge from the machine. Control is like that filter, where you still get an outcome from the relationship, but what you receive is only one of infinite possibilities.

People try to control their feelings, or control conversations (like Julie with Tom), or control their partner's actions out of jealousy, and all of it is based in fear. Fear is the Play-Doh filter where the only shapes it makes are ones that fall apart or just simply aren't fun. What makes relationships so scary is precisely because none of those things can really be controlled. Unless you hold that other person in actual slavery, then the component of free will means that you have zero control on the outcome. Oh, sure, you can *contribute* to a direction, to a path, but where you end up will be a mystery for both of you.

At one point, early on in our relationship, Midgie said to me, "I can't see it working out between us at some point. We're just too different." I told her I was amazed at her ability to accurately predict the future, to know that regardless of how it was working presently, that at some point, our relationship would cease to function. I pointed out that she knew neither who she would be at that "some point," nor who I would be. It was obvious to me that, for her, it was simply a way to control the outcome, to have a controlled exit from a relationship rather than a seemingly uncontrolled one in some fantasy future. I told Midgie that she had the freedom to leave at any point, and if that "some point" arrived where it did not work for her, then I would support her in whatever path she chose. Fortunately, since control was not an issue for me, it gave me space to make sure I could take care of all her concerns and set her on the right track.

It might actually be nice if control was more of an issue for me, so I could say more about it. Heck, I'm sure you're shaking your head knowing that most guys would probably have all sorts of control issues if there were other men sleeping with their lovers. Shoot, some men will get jealous if their lady even looks at a man with genuine appreciation. But, I know that those men get jealous and consequently become controlling because of the fear of their own inadequacy. Because I know the kind of man I am, I know that I don't have to fear anything from any guy. So you see, there's really no way for me to, like Dean, be blind-sided. I accept that Midgie is an independent person and I respect her judgment. Except with T.J. I don't know what in the Sam Hill she was thinking.

I guess the important thing about control is just that, when it comes to relationships, it offers nothing of real value. And if you want to get into the real meat of discovery in your relationships (or some kind of tasty bean if you're a vegetarian), then you have to learn how to let go. To allow yourself to follow the flow of an experience, like a surfer on a wave. You can't control where the wave will break; you can only point your surfboard in the direction that seems right and hope for the best. When you're first starting this process, you will fall again and again and again. It doesn't mean that you've failed. It means you are gaining more and more information about what it means to surf. And then, in a pivotal moment, you will ride that crest in a smooth arc all the way to shore.

Or I imagine it would be something like that if I

knew anything about surfing. The point is, that there are depths of what you can gain in a relationship that you haven't even begun to fathom, and you haven't even touched them because you're trying to *control* what you can gain, and because you don't know what you don't know, then what you can gain will be forever limited as long as you try to exercise that control.

It's like that *Matrix* movie. You've imposed a kind of control on yourself, and it doesn't matter if you learn everything about that reality you've constructed for yourself; that reality is not all that is or could be, so you really haven't touched anything. If you want to dive into the good stuff of relationships, the *really* good stuff, then you have to unplug from that reality you've constructed: what you think people are, what you think men offer, what you think women offer, and what you think relationships offer.

It's not about figuring out that other person. After you've done that deconstruction of all reality and you've poked your finger into a mirror that starts enveloping you, then you have to face the most fundamental question of all: why are you here? No, no, I don't mean one of those airy fairy pray-to-the-Universe-and-discover-your-ultimate-purpose kinds of things. That's what the

Dalai Lama would suggest, but we're talking relationships of the bumpy grindy variety, and to answer questions about that, then we need His Holiness Dalai Dr. Matt.

Why Have Relationships?

I talked a lot about intimacy when I was talking about sex, but I pointed out that sex was not the only path to it, nor was it automatically present when sex is present. Or, at least I meant to if I didn't. Either way, I figured I didn't really get enough into just what this intimacy business is, or why it's even important. I think that in order to do that, we need to first start talking about what relationships are for. We need to go all the way back to the genesis of relationships. Or at least to the book of Genesis.

Now, I wouldn't exactly call myself a religious man, but I do know an awful lot about the Bible. My fake doctorate wouldn't be worth much if I didn't look at how this pile of stuff called religion has influenced our perspective on relationships. Religion is pretty commonplace in North America, which is significant, so all those so-called educated people that dismiss it out of hand have a kind of willful ignorance that's impressive. That's not to say that the religious do not sometimes subscribe to willful ignorance, and sometimes they blame God for their idiocy, which to me is a kind of a spectacular display of egotism that makes me want to sit back and clap for the sheer audacity of it.

But putting that aside, there's a story that has permeated our culture beyond its religious roots, which is the story of Adam and Eve. Just to refresh your memory, in the story, Adam was a dude who was alone in the world. God and his partners (don't ask) decided that Adam needed a companion, so one day they put Adam to sleep, took out one of his ribs, and created a woman. That woman was named Eve.

Now, the story of Adam and Eve has been used as a metaphor—or even divine directive—to teach about a great many things, including love, companionship, trust, communication, betrayal, shame, heterosexuality, nutrition, and fashion.

It's also contributed to some unfortunate ideas, such as co-dependency, having only one true love, gender inequality, self-sacrifice, self-betrayal, sexual bigotry, and prejudice against snakes.

It's a simple story made complicated, or a complicated story over-simplified, and probably the two people most often betrayed in the telling of the story are the stars of it. Both of these people are new to the world, heck, even new as a species, so, chances are, they're going to make some pretty significant mistakes. Add onto that the fact that they are brand new to human relationships, and you're going to encounter some issues.

Put yourself in Eve's position. She wakes up and is told that she was created for this other fellow, and she hasn't even had an opportunity to date yet. Before she's even developed a sense of self, she's trying to offer herself to another person. And what happens if she were to leave the relationship? How do you move on with your life with the knowledge that there is one specific being out there who God, in all his wisdom, has stated that you are meant for? What do you tell the next guy? "Yeah, that's my ex-husband. We were created as a perfect match by God. But don't worry, honey, you're a great guy."

And then there's Adam. What if he sees the newly created Eve and decides that he's not attracted to her? She was made from his rib, so who exactly can he blame? Wouldn't he consider any rejection of her to be a judgment upon himself? And if she leaves, what then? It's not like he can ask God to keep cannibalizing all his ribs; that's completely unsustainable. At a certain point, you're going to need some ribs left to keep your guts in.

It wasn't a perfect scenario, but Adam and Eve do one smart thing, which is to use the relationship as a means for personal growth. Now, either one of them could have lived independently, and as they moved through the world, they would have grown. But there is an inherent limit to personal growth when one lives in isolation. The limit is that many of your experiences are still entirely dictated by your choice, and sometimes we only choose based on the experiences we already know. I'm not saying that a person who lives alone and out of intimate relationships cannot live a rich, full life, or that they can't be happy. After all, I have no doubt that my friend the Dalai Lama is a pretty happy guy. But, no matter how you slice it, what you can experience will only go so far, because you are only responding to the requests of your own free will.

What do I mean? Well, when you enter into the structure of a relationship, or create that structure, however you want to think about it, you have to let go of some of the control for what will transpire within that structure. You no longer entirely dictate all the terms. That doesn't mean you give up your free will, or abandon your boundaries, but your choices to bond with that other person means that the actions of that other person will have a profound effect on you. They are connected to your personal growth, and you may find yourself growing in ways you could not have anticipated on your own. Take a baby. I don't mean literally take a baby, but let's use a baby as an example. The fact that it is a being that is independent from you (even if they are, for a time, dependent on you), means that the effect of their existence on you is a complete unknown. It's an entirely unpredictable mystery, and for many people, this causes a great deal of discomfort.

In fact, many people end relationships or perhaps simply become distraught when they find themselves entering into an area of growth that is completely new and mysterious, and as a result, feel suddenly "out of control". Some people experience this when they enter in a relationship with someone who is very different than the typical person they've been in a relationship with. Others may misinterpret the sudden arrival into the unknown as being separated from or betraying their sense of themselves, instead of as a signal of significant growth that they may not be used to.

Now, folks, I don't want you to take what I just said as an automatic reason to act in ways that feel completely foreign to you. It's important to check back in with yourself and ask if what you're doing still lines up with who you are, even while recognizing that who you are is in a constant state of change. What I'm illustrating is the potential leaps and bounds in growth that relationships offer. Entering into a relationship that presents so much that is unknown is a tremendous act of courage, and two people choosing to move forward and communicate and be vulnerable with each other when the outcome is a mystery, embark on one of the greatest adventures I know. Folks, skydiving, climbing Mount Everest, and wrestling alligators are child's play compared to the courage and tenacity it takes to open to the full depth of all the possibilities in an intimate relationship. Most people are much more likely to drink snake venom in Thailand than fully open their heart to another human being, because the risk (or perceived risk) is so tremendous. Or because snake venom is incredibly tasty, I'm not sure.

Adam and Eve had a massive setback, when Eve took some poor spiritual and nutritional advice from a serpent, which ultimately resulted in the loss of their home. Their perfect world had been disrupted, and they had to find a new way to live, but they discussed the challenges presented to them, and grew into that new life together. The relationship, as a necessity, radically shifted from what they both had expected, but rather than complain, or blame each other for some unexpected hardships, they found a way to support each other into becoming people who could handle and overcome those hardships.

And then, to add insult to injury, one of their sons killed the other, and the death of a child is quite commonly an event which ends relationships. Yet Adam and Eve persisted. Sure, you could try and argue that the dating pool was still quite small in those days, but even living on their own would have been understandable considering the pain they necessarily needed to work through by staying together.

And that's just it, leaving each other would have afforded them a way to not have to move through their pain, or perhaps to move through it at a more comfortable, slower pace. So, no doubt those first few years after the death of their son had many moments of extreme discomfort. Yet the two partners continued to choose each other, to move deeper into their healing and their personal growth.

Folks, pay attention now, because everything I'm saying here is pure gold.

This is the reason for relationships, or perhaps the most important reason: **It creates growth beyond what a person may be able to achieve on their own.** This truth applies to all relationships, the bumpy grindy kind or not.

By the way, if you were thinking that perhaps

it's a little silly to take so much license with the story of Adam and Eve, I'd say I think it's important to figure out this story, because it's stories like this that get spread in people's consciousness and lead to certain beliefs that, in turn, lead to idiotic behavior. Maybe you haven't had a partner made for you using Divine Genetic Technology, but it's pervasive for people to think that there's one person out there that they are destined to be with. And certainly it's common when relationships end for people to think that no one else will ever again be so well-suited for them. Sometimes a person will be in a relationship, and will spend some time with a person other than their partner who seems to click with them in ways that they haven't experienced in their current relationship. And the thought will cross their minds: "Maybe *this* is really the person I'm supposed to be with."

Folks, let me set the record straight. God is not putting one particular partner on layaway, and waiting for you to walk blindly into them. Even people without religion have these stupid "romantic" ideals, including my atheist friend Roger. In the world of 21st-century dating, you would think that people have gotten smarter about it, but in some ways it's gotten worse. Now that people of both genders feel a lot more free to fully express their free-will, the choice to bond with one person in an intimate relationship has suddenly become more of a challenge. When it comes to that choice about whether or not to enter into a committed relationship, some people may say to themselves, "Have I fully explored all my options? Have I dated enough people? Is there someone more suited for me out there?"

Well, for those people, let me make this even more difficult for you.

1. *There are always more options to explore, and there always will be, so you will never explore all of them.*
2. *There is no limit on the number of people you can date, other than the time limit of your lifespan (and the willingness of other people). Also, there is no optimal number of people to date; and*
3. *Even if you're in a relationship, based on the law of probability, there is always someone out there more suited for you than your current partner.*

The last truth can make people uncomfortable, and that's why we interject ideas like divine intervention. We like to feel special and unique in the lives of our partners, and it's uncomfortable to think of someone else in that position and perhaps doing a better job of relating to our partner than we can.

But, by invoking divine intervention, or someone being uniquely qualified for the job as partner, we minimize the power of choice and free will. Our lives are driven by choice, and all choices, by definition, discard one or more options. If you only have one option that is truly "for you," then that's not much of a choice, is it? Hmm?

It's important for the third point above to be said, because a lot of people feel this but don't acknowledge it, and the knowledge that they hide from themselves comes out in a lot of unhealthy ways. Some people have affairs, some people never fully open to their partner, some resent the person they're with, and some drop their lover at the sign of any slightly better option. Midgie, for example, interprets this knowledge to mean that monogamy is an impossible scenario contrary to the way we actually feel. She points out that even previous examples of monogamy in nature that were held up to show the "natural" state of monogamy, were later shown by DNA testing to be false. Certain birds appeared to have life-long monogamous partners, yet the evidence showed that while they were socially monogamous, their sexual activities did not reflect the same. And let's not forget the bonobos, rubbing scrotums like they were shaking hands. Only with scrotums.

I don't mean to be contrary to Midgie, but I think using these behaviors as deterministic of what we should do demonstrates a lack of understanding in the value of choice. Think back to Adam and Eve. Just because they were genetically created explicitly *for* each other, it didn't mean that their lives were perfect, so the fact that they were a "perfect" match does not solve everything. Likewise, seeing an imperfect match and grabbing other imperfect matches to make up for it is still trying to create a perfect match, just using more pieces. What makes a relationship work has nothing to do with how perfectly the puzzle pieces fit together, and if you keep leaving relationship after relationship, or adding lover after lover in order to find that, then I'm sorry, you're going to have to get used to disappointment.

Let's say you had a "perfect" match right now, somewhere out there. That's right, they exist, and they're alive. Only thing is, your perfect match lives on the other side of the world, or is in a relationship they're not going to leave, or is maybe 50 years older than you and would therefore not be someone you would choose for other reasons. You might say,

"Well, c'mon, Dr. Matt, if they don't match my priorities or I wouldn't date them for some other social reason, then they're not really a perfect match." Well, *exactly*, you nincompoop, *you* decide who is perfect for you. God could create a whole line of partners for you using various bones and non-essential organs, and it still doesn't mean that any of them would work out. It's your own God-damned choice. It's completely arbitrary. You decide they are perfect for you, and they decide you are perfect for them, and *viola*, match made. It doesn't mean that the two of you are perfect, or that your puzzle pieces are 100% crafted by the gods using super-accurate lasers to align to one another. So get that stupid crap out of your head. If we are perfect in our imperfection (which we are), then it stands to reason that the relationship of two imperfect beings would be equally imperfect. And perhaps, just perhaps, that imperfection might be extremely important.

Pop used to say that the best friend to have is a blind midget, because you know they will never look down on you. He also used to say, "I never met a perfect person who wasn't, in some way, deceased."

But if your goal is still perfection, or to get near to perfection, then let's go back to muscle-building for a second. You could say that a perfectly intact muscle is one that has never been torn. Which means it is one that has never been worked, and therefore is completely weak. Yes, a muscle can be over-worked, and even torn in a way that causes irreparable damage, so be careful before you start reaching for imperfection just for its growth opportunities.

Have you ever met two people who seem to embody a perfect relationship? They never seem to have conflict with each other. Their lives and their relationship are constantly in a state of joy. For some reason, those people probably irritate you but you've never really thought about why. It seems judgmental to say they are too perfect. I met two people like that at a party once who wouldn't stop talking about how I needed to take yoga. They annoyed the crap out of me, and it's because the image they were projecting was a false one. I know they were not being real with each other, because they were not real with me. They didn't connect with who I was or what my interests truly were or how many books I'd written; instead, they seemed to have a need to thrust out the image of joy and perfection that they believed they possessed. For those kinds of people, I don't have much confidence in the strength of their relationship. Look, folks, if you have to go around telling people that you're enlightened, you're not there yet.

People have an idea that these perfect relationships exist, and therefore judge their relationships for their imperfections, or pretend they have perfection, or withdraw from intimate relationships altogether. Midgie's argument is that, because no one ever matches you perfectly, then you can't possibly learn all you need to learn about relationships from only one person. She does have good point. After all, to even place an expectation on another human being that they will meet all your relationship needs sounds extremely unfair. So why do it? Why choose just one, even if it is only one at one particular time? If you gain and learn from one person, wouldn't another person in the mix possibly offer you more in growth and knowledge? If we recognize the desire for some to have children, then do we judge people whose need or desire for children is not met by a single child? If we value our friendships, do we feel shame when one friendship offers something different but equally valuable to another friendship? Do we frown at the employee with multiple co-workers, or the entrepreneur with multiple business partners? Do we consider single parents to be able to give a deeper love then two parents because of their uniqueness in that child's life?

No? Then what exactly are we doing this mono-gamy thing for? These are the questions Midgie sometimes raises, and to be honest, I don't always know what to say to her. Except to basically shrug and say that the answer is choice. Monogamy is common because it's a common choice. She responds by saying that it's not choice if people have been raised to only consider one option as valid or moral. Similarly, says Midgie, if a pregnant girl in a religious household has been raised to con-sider abortion evil, or she is threatened with poverty if she makes that choice, then her choice to keep that child can't really be considered a choice at all.

Midgie makes strong arguments, and she's pas-sionate about what she says, but not all choices we make are between equally-balanced options. And whether or not one has been "indoctrinated," the expression of their free will is still up to them. One cannot say for sure that had they been raised differ-ently, they would have made a different choice. We all take societal expectations and moral and ethical guidelines into consideration in our choices. You can argue that Adam and Eve only stayed together because God had outright stated they were made for each other, but that assertion cannot be proven. It could be that Adam and Eve really dug each other, and might have stayed with each other even if God had said they were all wrong for each other. Of course, that decision would have been understandable. The Hebrew God in the Old Testament was not exactly consistent and was sometimes kind of a jerk. Or at least he was written that way. I mean, you think you have relationship issues because you have a jealous boyfriend? Try having a jealous God. But, that was a long time ago, and I'm sure if you met him in person he might be a totally cool guy. Of course, he'd have to first come to Earth as a human, and according to my Jewish friends, that hasn't happened yet.

I agree with Midgie that the choices of relationship structure are somewhat arbitrary and a matter of choice, and sometimes those options from which we choose are not equally informed. Perhaps monogamy was not so much a natural evolution but an imposed morality in order to control the expression of freedom as she suggests. One time I said to Midgie, "But don't you consider me a pretty well-informed person?"

"Well, of course," she said.

"Then why am I monogamous?" I said. "I would say I'm exposed to a lot of other options, wouldn't you?"

"Well..." Midgie said, thinking. "I wouldn't say

you're traditionally monogamous. Most monogamous people are controlling of their partner."

"Is it possible, Midge," I said, "that you're stereotyping monogamous people a bit?"

She smiled. "Well, I suppose it's *possible*."

"From what you've told me about polyamory, you're not strictly independent by those rules either, are you? I mean, you and I share a bank account."

She frowned. "That's just because it makes grocery shopping easier."

"And we own a truck."

"Well, I couldn't buy it on my own. What are you saying?"

"I'm not saying anything," I said, "but you don't share a bank account or own half a truck with anyone else."

This seemed to make Midgie a little bit uncomfortable, so I changed the topic. But I do sometimes think about what she has to say. For me, I just couldn't imagine trying to handle more than just Midgie. An intimate relationship takes time and energy, and multiple intimate relationships take more.

Think back to that child you picked up. The

truth is that a single child and single parent often *do* have a stronger bond than the parent-child relationship in a family with two adults and six children. But the single child might miss out on things like peer development with siblings, or inter-gender interactions between adults of different genders. I'm not saying one is better than the other, just that the types of relationships change as a natural consequence of our choices. With those two families, children in one environment might be gaining something that other children in different environments don't have.

All of these are related to choices, and choices are made from a nearly infinite number of options. Midgie's rationale to have multiple lovers seems to be based, in part, on the abundance of choice, but because options are nearly infinite, she's still paring down quite a bit. I've heard her say that she wants her freedom, but freedom and free will do not change based on our choices, unless we choose to stab someone in a bar fight and end up in prison. Therefore, to make an argument that one has less freedom by being monogamous or in a committed relationship is absurd. You still have all the freedom in the world.

When people talk about lack of freedom, what they're really talking about is consequence. Choices have consequences, and some consequences are unacceptable to you. Yet, still, this is a decision that you've made of a consequence you can't accept; it's not a lack of freedom that is inherent in the choice itself.

So don't worry, commitment-phobes. Making a choice to enter a long-term relationship does not mean that you give up your right to choice or abandon your free will. And if you find yourself going from relationship to relationship quickly to try to design or discover the perfect one, maybe find that guy or gal that has both perfect looks and perfect personality, then not only are you an insane person, but you may also be limiting your own growth. And because growth means that you have more freedom, then your avoidance of giving up freedom is exactly what is keeping freedom from you.

Why would only engaging in short-term relationships limit your growth? I'm glad you keep asking me these questions, because it certainly gives me more to write about. Well, in my last book, which is still one of the greatest books that one can find on the Internets, I talked about energy efficiency. I mentioned that in a nuclear reaction that generates power, one wants to have an optimal reaction which does not leave excess fissile material afterwards. I remember I heard a similar thing way back when I studied chemistry in a Texas high school. A rather frumpy teacher taught us about chemical reactions, and when making a new solution created from two components, he said you ideally wanted the precise amount of each component that would react and not leave anything left over.

In a relationship, you create solutions that are different from what each of you could create on your own. In fact, I've found that given the same sets of circumstances, two individuals working alone may find one ideal solution that is nearly identical, but working together, those same two individuals will often find a second, very different solution that they both agree is ideal. Midgie once posed the question of whether or not that meant that people in relationships are simply making decisions which they think will please the other person but which are not ideal for either of them. It's a good question, and that does happen sometimes, but it's not really what I'm talking about. Let's say that two hunters in 10,000 B.C., working alone, pose the question: "How long can I be out hunting?" The answer may be half a day. The two hunters team up and begin having great caveman sex, not necessarily in that order. Again, they ask themselves individually: "How long can I be out hunting?" They may be asking only about themselves, but the answer may be different, based on the fact that someone else may alternate tending to the fire, managing the caveman store, etc.

"Well, Dr. Matt, now you're just talking about the basic dynamics of teamwork," you're saying to me. Well, partly yes, it's in the category of teamwork, but the pair bonding that happens in relationships has dynamics all its own. Because it's not just about being able to do *more* of one task or delegating tasks amongst more people. It's also about creating possibilities which simply didn't exist with only one. We already know that this is true for reproduction, but the evolutionary dynamic which emerged for creating children still exists between two people when that's not happening. In other words, let's say that the creative force between two people exists whether or not a child manifests from that creative force or not. That creative force can be used and directed to create new solutions, just like the new solutions I created from two components in that chemistry class, if I remember correctly. I do remember that my high school chemistry teacher was not exactly widely-known for his excellent teaching skills.

Anyway, when you've only known someone for a short time, or only know just a little bit about

them, you don't know how much of what component to add. You create chemical reactions, but the
solutions tend to be smaller or last for a shorter
length of time. Not that these solutions are invalid;
it's just not the most energy efficient possibility for
you. Two people create leverage, and as they learn
about each other, they lengthen the lever. If you
know anything about levers, you know that it means
that the same energy input can create a greater
energy output. Now, if you're saying to yourself,
"That's not true at all and it has to do with how
energy is transferred and how force is applied blah
blah blah," then I'll point out that my high school
physics teacher was less impressive than my chemistry teacher. You can go on and on if you want, but
the long and short of it is that I've moved this pile
of rocks with my levers while you stood around
flapping your jaw. We can say that the apparent sub-
jective energy input is less with this handy dandy
lever.

You know what, though? It's not just a matter of
length of time. Two people can spend their lives
together and still create rather measly solutions. To
grow the size of those solutions, that takes something very specific. Yep, let's talk about what we've
been avoiding, that subject called "Intimacy."

Intimacy

Intimacy can be described in a few different ways: the willingness to be open and vulnerable, how much one shares with another, or how deeply you know about another person. So it is sometimes used to refer to a quality of a person, or the quality of the relationship. Intimacy is also described as something that two people enter into, a level of relating to each other that is different from how those people would relate to others.

However, this is my book, so we're going to describe it my way. We'll say intimacy is the size of the beaker. You know, the beaker in the chemistry set. Of course, beakers don't grow, so maybe that doesn't work so well. Intimacy is a tree that you water, that bears fruit. Hmm... I kill all my plants, so I don't know about that one, either. Intimacy is something that can grow, and its growth allows for greater and greater possibility. Are you thinking what I'm thinking? Yes, intimacy is exactly like James Cameron's Avatar.

Look, folks, I know we started off talking about *The Matrix*, but times change, and it's James Cameron who changes them.

James Cameron, if you don't know, is the director and imagineer of the brilliant otherworldly epic of *Avatar*, and is the same man who brought us *Titanic* and *The Abyss*. When he killed off Leonardo DiCaprio, he decided that he hadn't gone quite far enough in appealing to our fantasies, and dreamed up the world of Pandora. He then invested over ten years of his life to create it. That takes commitment, but I'm not going to talk about that quite yet.

What we're talking about is intimacy. Intimacy is a function of depth, not time. Folks, some other guy could have spent ten years on a project, and it could have been nothing more than macaroni art. Intimacy often naturally grows with time, but one can grow it consciously, and one can intentionally limit it from growth, no matter how much time is applied.

What Mr. Cameron was willing to do was to dive deeply into his dream, and explore everything that this dream held for him. Now, if you're thinking that what allowed him to do this was simply the money of a production company, I would challenge this belief. Because I believe that the man still had to stand in front of those individuals and unswervingly take a position that this was a world worth exploring. Simply making an investment of time or money does not create rich experiences. He had to personally believe in what was possible for himself. And what was possible for himself was a filmed story about giant blue people.

Just like the average relationship generally creates average intimacy, James Cameron could have said, "Okay, I'll simply tell my story about giant blue people in an average way." No one would have faulted him for that. It could have still been a grand adventure with lots of dragons and whatnot. He would have learned much from the experience, and could have easily built on that experience to create something later.

In other words, all of the steps would have been nearly the same. But he didn't simply stop there. He decided to push beyond the surface of each step, to create greater depth and a richness to the adventure he was seeking. And of course, that is why theatre billboards said "Avatar 3D" and not "Avatar Boring-D."

You may say that I haven't yet made this practical for you, but keep your pants on. First, I want you to understand that intimacy is a function of depth. *Avatar* in Boring-D I'm sure would be nearly identical with the movie in 3D. But one "feels" different from the other, or so I'm told. I wouldn't personally subject my eyeballs to a reduced experience. Anyway, the depth of an experience heightens the emotional impact of that experience. And the greater the emotional impact, the more that experience can create shifts and change for a person.

Intimacy is depth. It's not about what you do. Just like sitting in that theatre, the events portrayed on the screen in *Avatar 3D* and *Avatar Boring-D* do not change. The blue people don't touch ponytails more often. There aren't more dragons or six-legged horses. The ground doesn't glow more in that weird way when people walk on it. The events are identical, but the depth is greater with one than the other.

So, what does this mean for you? First, it means that if you avoided seeing *Avatar* in theaters until it was gone, then I feel sorry for you. But more importantly, it means that intimacy is not about having sex more often (although, in general, people should), and it's not about communicating more with each other, although that couldn't hurt. These may *bring* greater intimacy, don't get me wrong. In fact, never get me wrong. But that's not what intimacy is. Intimacy is about the depth of those experiences, how connected one feels during that sexual act, or how honest and open one is while communicating. We all know that the words, "I love you," can have a wide diversity of meaning and impact depending on the person and the situation. Greater intimacy provides a greater depth.

Obviously, if I'm saying that nothing about the situation needs to change, neither the words nor the actions, you may be wondering just where the heck you put the intimacy. How can one create greater intimacy without a change in action? Without you saying to that other person, "Let's do this or that differently?"

The answer is so simple you're going to kick yourself for not thinking of it. The answer is that you put on your 3D glasses.

Hmm, maybe that's not quite as simple as I thought it would be. Let me explain. When you're sitting in that theatre seat and there's this story about inexplicable floating rocks unfolding in front of you, the only participation required by you is your choice and willingness to wear the 3D glasses, which alters your perspective and creates a deeper experience.

Look, folks, you know I hate metaphors, so I sympathize if this one is confusing. Certainly, in your life, you have no 3D glasses to wear, and they really wouldn't be useful in a relationship even if you had them. But everything else can pretty much stay the same. We leave the glasses in their little plastic package, and all that's required is your choice and willingness to alter your perspective by degrees and create a deeper experience.

You see, there's nothing on the screen in front of you that can create a greater depth. The depth created is proportional to your mutual participation. If you do nothing, if you just abandon your ability to see what's in front of you, then all you get is an unwatchable double-image with some exciting sounds. I mean, you may experience *something*, but surely not everything that experience has to offer.

And, what, exactly, does intimacy offer you, you ask? Well, if you were paying attention at all, I already told you. Intimacy increases the potential power output of two individuals, without requiring an equal energy input. You may ask yourself, "Self, how is this possible? How can I get a greater energy output without an equally greater energy input?"

Well, I suppose that since we've used all the material on the surface to create our chemical reactions, and the solutions in intimacy become greater than the sum of their parts, then we have to dive deeper than chemical reactions into sub-atomic ones. Without intimacy, we could try to perfect our solutions all we want, and, like regular teamwork, you can produce a near-perfect solution. But what you haven't done is release any of the stored energy in the atoms themselves. Yes, intimacy is the ultimate Nuclear Option.

Like any nuclear option, intimacy must be approached with some care. A wrong move or carelessness and it can produce a devastating energy. It's no wonder that so many people are afraid of it, including you. Some people would rather go their whole lives avoiding creating brilliant and unbelievable solutions for themselves because, to some, mediocrity is a better solution than potential devastation. They don't realize that this is ultimately self-defeating and idiotic. Seeking mediocrity as a way to avoid pain is a pointless exercise because a) pain will likely find you anyway, and b) you're just doing it to create the illusion of control when, in fact, you have very little.

Now you're saying: "Dr. Matt, you haven't left me with much choice. Pursue intimacy, and I may end up devastated, or acquiesce to mediocrity and I will end up defeated." Good, I'm glad you see it that way too, because I didn't want to be the only one. You're right. One solution has little or no gain, but less risk, and one has more risks and the potential gains are tremendous.

I absolutely understand if you don't want to dive

into intimacy, because cowardice is quite common, especially if you've been hurt before. Many people avoid intimacy their entire lives, even while being in relationships. In fact, sometimes, you can find two people spending their days together where intimacy is the last thing on their minds. And they aren't necessarily miserable, but they're probably about as lively as a couple of fenced-in buffalo.

I'm not telling you how to live your life. I'm just pointing out that you've been living your life like an idiot.

You see, Einstein had it right, with his energy equation. Except Dr. Matt would put it like this:

$$E=i^2p^2$$

That is, energy equals the square of the depth of intimacy times the square of the number of participants. Folks, do you have any idea what you can create out of such a force? I want to point out at this point that intimacy is not an exercise limited to two people. You can create intimacy with just yourself, and you'll still have a higher energetic yield when you increase your depth of intimacy.

Midgie pointed out after reading this over my shoulder that polyamorous triads or larger groups have a greater energetic output using that formula. Perhaps, but I pointed out that intimacy depth is also a squared number, and one has to consider how deep the intimacy can reach in that scenario. If you have a dozen people participating in amorous relationships with each other, then the depth of intimacy may be limited purely as a matter of logistics. In fact, if I may clear that up a little further, since Midgie's comments have brought up polyamory a few times, I'd say that my observation has been that you don't really get one "large" relationship in polyamorous situations. What you really have are concurrent relationship pairs. In fact, the only difference between serial monogamists and the polyamorous really is just timing.

Each relationship bridge between two people is unique. Therefore, the maximum number of participants in that formula really is just two. So, if you are in two concurrent relationships, then you end up with:

$$E=i^2 2^2 + s^2 2^2$$

...with s being the second depth of intimacy. We can also write this as:

$$E=4(i^2 + s^2)$$

Before you see the greater multiplication factors, remember this is just energy output, and you have to consider your energy input. If, for you, the depth of intimacy would shrink with an added relationship, while increasing your energy input, then you may end up with a net loss. As you know from reading my book, *Just Stop Having Problems, Stupid!*, considering your overall energetic loss or gain is essential for effective decision making.

On the other hand, Midgie could have a point. It's possible the energy structure of a group could equal the energy structure of two individuals, just in a different way. I mean, we know this is possible because of our simple formula, and we know the formula is right because I made it. But I don't know exactly how that works for Midgie, but it does seem to work somehow.

What I do know is that the energy dynamics of multiple pairs are not equal with affairs. Let's consider an affair. Really consider it. I mean, look at how tantalizing that new person looks. That is just a beautiful, exciting being on this earth. It's possible that the intimacy level of this affair could be fantastic. Now, after you've stopped fantasizing, let's look at the facts.

Here's the obvious: you may end your pre-existing relationship. Is it because the energy requirements for an affair are high? No, it's because you've broken trust and trust is a necessary foundation for long-term relationships. Let's be honest here. The energy output formula is the same for affairs. A relationship is a relationship. So, you may well indeed create brilliant solutions, and you may find truths and powerful outcomes from that new relationship, but your existing relationship has now been soured by deception. Because of your intimate connection, you'll continue to create powerful outcomes, but now you're injecting an energy of a most disastrous nature.

You see, not all intimacy is positive. And since you bring it up, let's talk about it, because this next topic is, by far, the biggest area where people act like the most amazing idiots of all.

Break-ups

Boy howdy, if there's one thing that people don't do well, it's break-ups. There's another person who they've stated that they love and wish to treat with respect, and then proceed to treat that person with the most disrespect that they've ever treated another human being. And as if that wasn't the most idiotic part, most people, especially in their youth, are sometimes proud of their own despicable behavior, as if being scorned by a lover was an automatic license to forego any sense of their own moral and ethical center, and succumb to a vileness usually reserved for bully characters in '80s films. Or, if you like more modern films, it's the behavior of hardened security personnel who have been too long in a world they don't appreciate, and have begun seeking ways to destroy it. (See: *Avatar* and *The Matrix*.)

Why are people such jerks during break-ups? Have you ever asked yourself this question? If not, go ahead and ask it. I'll wait...

... Did you come up with any answers? If you've been listening to me long enough, you may have a few theories. You might suggest that it's because people are often hurt, and people who are wounded act out. Sure, but that's only part of the story. Why does it sting *you* so much? Even after a bit of time, one little thing said by that other person can hurt deep, or send you into a rage, where you throw your espresso machine against the wall and tear out a piece of your mustache. But why?

Well, let's go back to the bridge. You've built a bridge with this other person. Sex maintains the bridge, and intimacy strengthens it, yet lack of sex and intimacy does not necessarily tear it down. When you break up with someone, the bridge is still there, and, rest assured, your bridge looks like crap. The beams are broken, the asphalt is cracked, the cables are frayed, and you'd be crazy to drive on it, but it's there. And now it's hosting colonies of pigeons. There are enough pigeons that they have started specializing; they've converted from hunter-gatherer to farming, and some of the pigeons have begun to ponder the wonders of the Universe. If anything, it's the pigeons that are holding the bridge together with layers of pigeon crap. They mingle aimlessly, go about pigeon tasks, and coat your bridge with another layer of crap.

That sounds pretty disgusting, doesn't it? Well, good, because you've been leaving these bridges all over the place, and I'm tired of seeing your crappy pigeon havens. I mean, aren't you? For one thing, it limits the spaces where you can put a nice bridge, and even if you do manage to put a nice one in, it's probably going to look upon the old crappy one. Doesn't that piss you off? On a long enough timeline, you can't even *have* a nice bridge. Not really. You've run out of good views, good spaces, and good foundations.

So, what can we do about those bridges? Well, dismantle them.

Aha! Here's where you get caught. You're thinking to yourself, "What else can I do? I've cut off all ties with that jerk. I don't ever speak to them. I've squelched all hope of a future relationship. Dr. Matt, why do I still have a bridge with poopy pigeons?"

Yes, why indeed? It doesn't sound logical to you, yet you unsurprisingly know that what I say is true. You can almost hear the pigeons fluttering about on your old bridge, taunting you with their poop.

Here's the problem. Treating someone like a jerk, or ignoring them, does not tear down one of these bridges. Love and intimacy created this bridge, and only love and intimacy can dismantle it. Now, before you start complaining, I'm not suggesting you go get some final make-up sex and call the whole thing even. That's stupid. I'm explaining the nature of bridges, so just pay attention.

Intimacy, you see, does not cease when you end a relationship. It transforms. What it transforms into depends entirely on your collective input. As the product of two people, it's easy for the resulting energy output to be destructive, but it doesn't lose its power ratio. Intimacy, in the short term, remains a constant, but the quality of intimacy is a negative one. If two powerful people decide to become negatively intimate, then the resulting output of negativity follows the same energy formula:

$$E = i^2 p^2$$

A friend told me the other day that people in love can move mountains. It's the same for people who are negatively intimate, only it's via an explosive volcano that covers the countryside and kills all the villagers. You know exactly what I'm talking about, because you've seen it happen. The relationship explodes, and it's not just the couple that gets hurt, but that negativity seems to land everywhere.

And folks, be clear that I'm not talking about grief. Or anger. Or any of the other range of emotions that come up and are healthy to feel. There's a true loss, and it's normal to feel those things. I'm talking about bona fide dickish actions, actions which are intentionally hurtful and without integrity. And not just actions, but also the negative feelings about the person in general: judging them when you think about them, and hoping that retribution will come to them even if you would never dream of doing it to them in person. (Because you're nice, after all.)

You're focusing your energy on that person whenever you hold such grudges, and every moment that you do, you release a pigeon. And that pigeon flies over to the bridge you built with that person, and poops on it, and then starts living out its life there.

I suppose the only upside to this is that your former lover is probably also releasing pigeons, but I'm not sure that that's much of an upside.

Look, pigeons are stupid. You're probably putting as much thought into releasing them as they're putting into toileting locations. Pigeons aren't altogether destructive, but they don't exactly create a pleasing aesthetic where they hang out, and together, a colony of pigeons consumes a lot of energy. Step one is that you stop releasing your pigeons, and because your lover may still be releasing theirs, step two is that you dismantle the bridge. As I said, both steps are done using love and intimacy.

Before I tell you just how to dismantle that bridge, let's look at how relationships end in the first place. I almost wrote, "Let's look at how relationships go wrong," but sometimes there's nothing wrong with a relationship ending, so it's a good thing that I didn't write that. On the other hand, we're assuming that relationships actually end. I'm sure that last sentence is a little confusing for some of you, but we'll get to that later.

Let's get back to Dean, the guy whose girlfriend had dumped him for a ski instructor. Dean had come to my apartment / office a few times to give me money so I could tell him what to do. The second visit after his break-up, he was still down in the dumps.

"I feel like I just got bulldozed, Dr. Matt," he said to me. I found this to be a bit of exaggeration, since the feeling of being bulldozed would likely be a kind of bone-crushing sensation that leads to one's death. He continued: "It just makes me angry. It wasn't right what happened, and I'm going to get to the bottom of it."

"Anger is good, Dean," I said. "It's an important part of the process. But, are you sure you know what you're angry at?"

He frowned at me. "What do you mean?" he said.

"Well, it sounds to me like you think you were a victim," I said.

"Of course," said Dean. "I didn't do anything wrong."

"Dean," I said, "why would you think that you would have to do something wrong for someone to leave a relationship? Who says it has anything to do with you?"

That seemed to stop Dean in his tracks, so I elaborated a bit more. I didn't want to elaborate too much, because I was thinking of seeing that *District 9* movie which was out at the time, and whenever I looked at Dean, I could only think about alien weaponry. But, anyway, I continued: "People leave relationships for their own reasons, and even the reasons aren't so important. In fact, the reasons are usually stupid. What's important is that she has free will, and so do you, and this time she exercised it in a way that you didn't like. It's not more personal than that. She made a decision that you wouldn't have."

"But Dr. Matt, even my friends say this was wrong," he said, still giving me that I'm-a-victim voice.

"Listen, Dean, I'd beware of your friends' statements about the relationship if I were you. They love you, and they don't like to see you hurt, but they weren't in the relationship. So they reach for the closest thing they can think of, which was when they feel they were wronged in a relationship. I'm not saying they're right or wrong; I just think you should stick to your feelings and not theirs."

Dean ran his hands through his hair, thinking about this, and that movement of his arm made me think of that scene in the movie preview for *District 9*, where the robot reaches up to grab a rocket. I glanced at the clock, noting that I still had some time, so I kept talking.

"Relationships are interesting. When you come to a road block, say one that has been put up in an internment camp for aliens, then either you both go around it, or neither of you go around. If only one of you goes around it, perhaps because you see some fresh raw meat on the other side, then you're no longer in the relationship."

"Uh, I don't understand, Dr. Matt," said Dean.

I could see that Dean still had a lot of work to do. "The point is, Dean, that you walked a pretty long distance on that road together. As a result, you, personally, are a lot further along that road than you were, and so is she. Be grateful for it."

Dean looked confused. "But… am I still in an alien internment camp looking for raw meat?" I thought he posed an excellent question, a question I wanted answered by that evening, so I ended our session.

I called up Midgie and we tried to see that *District 9*, but it was all sold out. Midgie suggested seeing *Harry Potter*, which I did not want to see, but I convinced myself that not wanting to see something was not a big issue when it came to enjoying the pleasure of another person's company.

But anyway, let's talk a little more about where relationships go wrong. Some of you may be saying, "But Dr. Matt, I've never had a relationship go wrong." Okay, your relationship may be much different. Maybe you had an "amicable split" as they say, and no one was hurt, and everyone lived happily ever after. You never harbored resentment or felt regret, and both of you acted like adults and held each other in high regard as you expressed your gratitude and went on your separate ways. You, sir or madam, are an exemplary and enlightened individual, and it's wonderful to meet someone who has risen above petty human emotions to achieve something closely resembling the amazing relationships of highly-developed robots, sort of like the courtship one might expect to see between a Roomba and the disembodied Einstein-bot.

So, I guess we won't be talking to you right now. You can sit back and relax, and I'll address the others present: people who make mistakes in the course of negotiating relationships with humans, and then go on to have feelings about it.

Other people who are present: I'm sure you're asking yourself, "So why is it that relationships so often end idiotically? Why is it that two people who begin with love for each other sometimes end up acting like morons to each other?" I'm glad you're asking these questions, because you're one of those people who has acted like an idiot, and it's nice to see that you're starting to develop some self-awareness. We've made a lot of progress in this book so far, you and I. You've come further and further in understanding your idiotic behavior and how to correct it, and I've come closer and closer in writing these chapters to being done with this book and getting to some blockbuster book sales.

Bear in mind, I'm not saying you are an idiot; I'm saying you've *been* an idiot. There's a difference. You've acted like an idiot, and you have an opportunity to not act like an idiot next time.

Perhaps you're uncomfortable with the fact that I keep talking about your idiotic behavior. Oh, I see. You just wanted to know about the *other* person's idiotic behavior. Maybe you didn't read the title of this book carefully enough. There's really no reason to talk about the other person, because people usually have a long list of what the other person did wrong that led to the end of the relationship, but they sometimes struggle to come up with the list with what they themselves did wrong. Luckily, I'm here to help.

First, let's take a few things off your list that may have been put on by other people. It wasn't that you never picked up after yourself. It wasn't that you left the toilet seat up or the cap off the toothpaste. It wasn't that you were too angry, or that the only time you were actually nice was when you were drunk. It wasn't that you never shared your feelings, or weren't compassionate enough. It wasn't because you were a flirt, and it wasn't because you were a cold fish in the sack.

Those aren't the things that go on your list, so let's go ahead and take those off. That isn't what you did wrong. None of those things are what causes relationships to end. What causes relationships to end is the same thing that causes them to start: choice. This is exactly as I explained it to Dean. People choose to not continue on a path with another person (or think that they can't because they perceive something is in the way), and that is essentially what we call the end of the relationship. Oh, they can attribute it to X, Y, and Z all day long, but at the end of the day, the path ahead seemed more appealing without that other person next to them than with them.

There could have been a different outcome. They could have liked the bear-cave-like feeling of clothes on the floor. They could have liked toilet seats in the upright position. They could have had paranoia about toothpaste caps. They could have loved the party scene and loved the drunkard who entertained. They could have hated discussing feelings. They could have valued their feeling of independence and your honesty when you were attracted to others and not only them. They could have appreciated a really chilled fish.

Were any of those things true, the outcome of the relationship might have been different. But what they decided was what actually worked in their life, and your quirks perhaps turned out to not be amongst what worked. But that's okay, because what works for them has nothing, really, to do with you, other than you may have helped them discover themselves, and in their discovery, they gained clarity about what it was they truly wanted.

Other times, people get scared. They're shown what's possible, and they get scared of that possibility. Sometimes it's because they don't know how they would handle it. Sometimes it's because you seem to represent a huge change to their life and they're afraid of that change.

No, I'm not letting you off the hook entirely. It's possible you acted like an idiot. In fact, I guarantee you acted like an idiot. I'm just pointing out that attaching idiocy as the reason for the end of the relationship is an explicit statement that the relationship's end is idiotic. And if both people accept this idiotic premise, then idiotic behavior will ensue on both sides.

What needs to be recognized is that relationships end out of choice, and we can leave all the idiotic attachments out of it. We can withdraw it from the equation, and we are therefore left with the simple formula for why relationships end:

$$R = \sqrt{(p^2 c^2 \Delta + m_0^2 c^2)}$$

So, now that you understand that, let's get back to dismantling that bridge. I told you that only love and intimacy were going to bring that old thing down, and I meant it. The problem is that you've been so obsessed with how to get rid of the bridge that you've neglected entirely to look at where the bridge is anchored and where you got the materials to build the bridge in the first place.

Isn't it obvious? The bridge spans all the way right to you, my friend. Where else did you think that your end of that bridge was located? It's anchored right there in your chest cavity. And you certainly know that you invested yourself in the building of that bridge, how could you not? So those parts of yourself that you invested were part of the building materials. You can't just tear the bridge down. You'd be dragging pieces of bridge everywhere you go. And you can't just abandon the bridge. There are pieces of you in that bridge, and if you start leaving pieces of yourself everywhere, you're not going to have much of a self left.

Don't you get it? The only solution is not to demolish the bridge but to transform the bridge into something else. And I don't mean just take those beams and immediately build another bridge, that's just stupid. You have to get inside those beams to get all of the you out, melting down that structure into its base elements where they can be safely separated into rock and steel. But, of course, when you build a bridge, some of those materials are imports. I don't want you to get the impression that you only use yourself to build bridges, just that you invest yourself into it. That's not a bad thing, people, that's just the nature of bridge building, and once you understand it, you can manage it safely.

So, with all the extra materials on hand, there's more than you can reclaim all for you. You've imported some of the materials from the world around you, and it's not so easy to find the original shipping containers and send it all back. And, really, no one is asking for it back. It's a gift, so don't worry about it. What you really want to do is to reclaim what is yours, and then build a new structure using the remaining material.

Separating this material can take a bit of work. You have to figure out exactly what's yours, what's the other person's, and what's material you can build from. (Just be sure to wash off all the pigeon poop, because that stuff is about as worthless as the creatures who left it.) It's pretty delicate work considering that you're doing this stuff right there in the ol' chest cavity. You have to know yourself in order to recognize yourself in these materials, and that kind of knowledge of self is called intimacy.

When you've separated the materials, then what do you build? It can be a library, a temple, a statue, whatever the heck you want. Heck, it can still represent the relationship, just not the structure that was no longer serving you. The only way you're going to know is to ask yourself questions about what you want. It's a process called communication.

I'm sure you've realize that even though you haven't done this process consciously, there are people from your past who you've managed to get over. So, this rebuilding can happen pretty naturally, if you'll just get out of the way and let the construction workers do the job. It requires you letting go of control.

All the while, you're still building in the chest cavity, and that means that these structures are going to necessarily be close to your heart. And it should be fairly obvious that building close to your heart requires love.

Communication, letting go of control, and the most important ingredients: intimacy, and love.

Now that I've revealed the Secret of the Key, I'm sure one question is on your minds: What happened to the pigeons? Well, the advantage of a closed chest cavity is that it should be inaccessible to pigeons. Hopefully, they died of starvation and we should never speak of them again.

The second question you have is: What happens with the other side of the bridge, and the bridge materials that aren't mine? I wouldn't worry too much about that either. Any extra materials that you don't claim or build out of are returned to the other person. And then, it's up to them if they want to build something new or do nothing and drag half a bridge with them. The favor you've done for them is that you've already cut the bridge cables, and that's one less task for them on a possible path of being more constructive.

With all this work I'm describing at the end of relationships, maybe this is making you even more terrified of relationships in general. But, look, you were gifted a lot of the material for the bridge, so whether you realize it or not, you ended up with more than when you started, and hey, you got a free art museum out of it in the end. Experiences of this nature are overall a net gain. "Wait, Dr. Matt, what about extremely negative relationships? Not just your idiots but your full-on assholes?" Well, of course I'm not saying to engage in those relationships because of the learning experience, and what you get to build afterwards. But the fact that you are asking the question means that you *did have* that learning experience. Your knowledge of yourself potentially increased a tremendous amount, and that means that the material you have to build from after that is equally tremendous.

Your question is really trying to be a justification for your fear, and you don't realize that your fear is more about that historical pain than future potential pitfalls. Even all this talk about bridges probably makes you uncomfortable, let alone that I said sex was at all involved in the maintenance of an intimate relationship bridge. I'm sure you'd love to have relationships devoid of bridges, and just have completely autonomous pillars of independence, but that's sort of like having two cities who become trading partners without building any roads between them—before airplanes had been invented, of course—or boats or submarines if the cities are on the water—plus, horses haven't evolved and the only communication is carrier pigeons, which everyone shoots on sight.

The point is a relationship *is* a bridge. Bridges and roads in human history have led to the spread of knowledge and the evolution of societies. Yes, bridges also sometimes bring Trojan horses and rampaging barbarians, but the solution is not to burn all your bridges and hide behind the castle walls for the rest of your life. You can try if you want, but good luck not going crazy.

The trick instead is to build solid, stable bridges. And protect those bridges with guard towers and night watchmen. And for the love of God, don't let pigeons nest there because they will crap your bridge up in no time.

In other words, it's not enough just to build a bridge. You've built a bridge out of good materials, and sex and intimacy may strengthen the bridge, but that doesn't make your bridge invulnerable. If only sex and intimacy were required to maintain a bridge, then they'd probably never fall apart, or get covered in pigeon crap.

Bridges take a maintenance plan that extends beyond sex and intimacy; that is, if you choose to have the continued existence of a solid, stable, and pigeon-free bridge. It's a choice of a different order, not a choice made at a single point in time, but the culmination of infinite choices along the life of your bridge. There are a series of choices that you're making constantly, and chances are, you're not aware how often you're making them. How little you know about these choices is not the smartest, but fortunately I'm here to straighten you out. We put your road into the third dimension with intimacy, and now we're going to take it into the fourth dimension with time.

Hmm... maybe I didn't give my high-school physics teacher enough credit.

Hold that thought, because Midgie's home. That's good, because I'm ready to close off this topic of break-ups, and it's not really that applicable to the moment anyway.

The Despair of the Unknown

Well, folks, Dr. Matt is feeling a bit rough right now. You see, that night, Midgie arrived home as always. She had been out with our good friend Kate that evening, so as she put her jacket away, I asked how her time with Kate was. I was a little surprised by what happened next.

"The evening was interesting," she said. "We should probably talk about it."

"Oh?" I said. Whenever Midgie says something like that, I know I should probably pay attention.

"Kate came onto me," she said.

I chuckled. "Well, that's pretty bold for Kate. I never even knew she--"

"We made love," said Midgie, abruptly.

I stopped chuckling. "Excuse me?" I said.

"I know. I was pretty taken aback by how bold she was, too."

"Midgie, that's not what I mean. I mean, I thought you were just out as friends," I said.

"We were," she said. She frowned, "Are you upset with me? I've had other lovers before."

"Other lovers?" I said. "You make it sound like this is the start of a new relationship."

"Well..." she said, sheepishly. "It *was* pretty fantastic. And I love Kate a lot."

"Hold the cow horns," I said, sitting down. "Midgie, this isn't about other lovers. This is about you going out the door with a friend and coming back with a new relationship, and this being the first I'm hearing about it. Plus, this is Kate. Did you stop to think about the fact that it might be weird if you started dating an ex-lover of mine?"

This startled Midgie. "Oh! I never even thought about it. I mean, we've all been friends for a while, I'd forgotten about that."

"Well, that seems convenient," I said.

"What are you saying? I wouldn't ignore your feelings just to get laid. I didn't know that it would be awkward for you."

"You also didn't ask me, Midge."

She sighed. "I know. I'm sorry. It's just that I've

been with other women before, and it's never seemed to bother you. In fact, you've usually seemed to like the idea, even though you strangely turn down the invitation to be present."

"Look, a woman being with another woman I can get behind. I've always stated that publicly. And you know how I feel about simultaneous sharing. I don't like to split my focus."

"Well, couldn't it be focused on you? Come on, why don't you challenge yourself when it comes to sex?" she said.

"Midgie, this has nothing to do with the issue, and this is enough of a challenge already. I don't want you to be with Kate."

"What does that mean?" she said.

"It doesn't work for me."

Midgie seemed at a loss for words. "Well, then if I want to be with her..."

"...then you can't be with me," I said immediately, completing her sentence.

Now, folks, I didn't cover ultimatums in the last chapter about break-ups, but they certainly are a quick path to ending a relationship. And in a short time, I had done just that.

The crazy thing is, I don't know which part had gotten me so upset. I had certainly never really talked to Midgie like that.

But that was it. That wasn't the exact end of that particular conversation, but it certainly didn't get any better from there.

Crap.

For the last month, Midgie's been staying at her dear Mom's place, to give us both space. Space for what? You'd think I'd know. I mean, for Pete's sake, I'm the Most Famous Fake Doctor Of Our Time™. I give advice on these things all the time.

Hmm... time. That's where we left off last. And space. It sounds like where I was getting to with fourth dimensions, but I'm not sure exactly where to pick that up now.

Here's the rub about the space-time continuum. Say you're important. Say you're important enough to be a planet. No, wait, say you're important enough to be a star. The truth is that no matter how big of a star you are, you're mostly surrounded by empty space. That's right, you're about as isolated and alone as one can get. And if you got too close to some other body, then you'd probably incinerate it long before it got close enough to touch. How's that for fourth-dimensional space-time?

Folks, forget relationships. The truth is that you're drifting in space, alone, and you'll stay that way until you explode or collapse in on yourself.

Commitment

Upon reading a draft of the previous chapter, my editor suggested that I might want to chop it out. I told her that I have no regrets, and cutting sections out while editing is just a way of expressing regrets. She feels a bit differently about it, but I'm the one writing the checks.

Another month passed with me thinking that the world had just ended. But, at the same time, I was thinking about some other things that Midgie had said.

You see, our conversation hadn't ended with my misguided ultimatum. It probably would have been ideal if we had stopped sooner rather than later, because things started to get fired up. That's when you start throwing in things that have nothing to do with the conversation.

For example, at one point, Midgie randomly brought up how I've been around lovers. I protested. "Midgie, I don't understand, I've never been against you having other lovers."

"Maybe, but you act like such an alpha dog around them. It's like you want to make sure they know you rule the roost. You intimidate people. The only person you didn't was T.J."

"T.J. was a jackass," I said.

"I know he was a jackass, and it was a bad idea to ever date him," she said, "but that's not the point."

"I made friends with Roger."

"Yes, but you still made sure he knew that I was always coming home to you," she said, "which is stupid, because of course I'm coming home to you. Maybe you didn't do it overtly, but it's still like you want to control the outcome. But don't you think by now I can make up my own mind?"

This baffled me. After all, I've always supported Midgie's independence. Midgie's fierce independence has always been a great attraction to me. Midgie's got spirit. And spunk. She's a force of nature. Although, I suppose "force of nature" is not the best phrase, because nature is so unpredictable in a way that's terrifying, and certainly I wouldn't be terrified of Midgie.

As I said, the conversation left us both drained, and Midgie and I decided on a little time apart.

Of course, this was unfortunate, because I was about to finish writing this book about relationships, and my only chapter left was this one, about commitment. Talking about commitment after potentially ending a relationship seemed awkward. I mean, we weren't exactly committed to each other. We'd been living fairly independent lives. I'd been traveling around the world, doing interviews, signing books, and often Midgie was with me, but not always. She'd been doing her lectures and workshops, and hosting the occasional sensual party.

But, folks, as you know, whether or not I'm qualified to talk about something doesn't prevent me from quickly establishing my expertise. Commitment was not so elusive as to be unattainable.

However, I knew I wasn't going to get any closer to the answer by just moping around, so after a few weeks of that, I decided to call up one of my good friends, famous architect Jonathon Stembridge-Rickenbacker. If you've visited my blog or listened to my podcast (which would only make sense that you have), you'd know that I talk to JSR on a regular basis. Strangely, though, he and I had not spoken for some time.

If I haven't told you before, Jon's relationship history is unique. He was divorced, and two years after being divorced, remarried the same woman.

Some would see this as one of the crazier ideas that one could do, but if you spend time with the married couple, I dare you to not be impressed with the quality of their relationship.

You might ask yourself how this is possible. I think a lot of people would make the assumption that if a couple were married and then divorced, then a second marriage would probably be doomed to the same fate. Yet, year after year, Jon and his wife challenge this assumption, and continue to strengthen and build their relationship.

I met Jon at one of my favorite establishments that makes the best soy lattes. If you're ever in Vancouver, stop by Caffe Artigiano. Seriously, no one makes a better soy latte anywhere. If you're not a fan of soy, or things that taste good, then go to Starbucks.

Jon and I both ordered lattes and sat down. We chit-chatted for a bit, and I told him about the conversation with Midgie.

"Wow," said Jon after listening. "So how are you doing?"

I shrugged. "Well, I wouldn't say I'm ready to ride a bull at a rodeo, but I'm doing okay right now."

"Are you still talking to Midgie?"

"We've chatted on the phone," I said. "I think she's feeling a bit guilty about Kate."

Jon shook his head. "Our dear Kate. This is a bit of a situation."

"That's for damn sure," I said.

Jon cocked his head and looked straight at me. "So, you never told Midgie that you still had a crush on Kate?"

I frowned. "Of course not, what would be the point of that?"

"And I suppose you never said that to Kate either?"

I shook my head. "No, I stopped flirting with Kate a long time ago, certainly after I was with Midgie."

"Well, not to flirt," Jon said, "I just mean..."

"That I could have prevented this situation?" I said, raising an eyebrow.

"No, not exactly. Midgie still has free will."

I nodded. "That's true. And it's her free will I respect. I've always been impressed with the choices that Midgie makes, especially how daring she is."

"Yeah," said Jon. "There's definitely no one else like Midgie."

"Absolutely," I said. "A lot of people don't get her at first. When you're that out there and visible promoting sexual exploration, people tend to judge, especially because they have so much judgement and shame around sex for themselves."

"Do you feel you get judged by being with her?" asked Jon.

"I'm sure it happens from time to time. Perhaps a stranger hearing our story would have judgements about our relationship. They might not even realize that, since they don't really know us and aren't *in* the relationship, then their judgements only reveal their own relationship issues. Midgie's friends were initially quite a bit apprehensive about me, or perhaps our relationship. It went as far as staging an intervention."

Jon laughed. "How did that go?"

"You know Midgie," I said. "She wasn't pleased at having her choices questioned. Her friends fortunately survived the incident."

"And how did you feel about it?" my friend asked.

"Well, look, when you're in a relationship long enough, things come up that will potentially negatively impact it. Pigeons can fly in from anywhere and land on the bridge you built, and it's better to just get those flying rats off your bridge rather than try to go lecture the person who released them. After all, sometimes their bridges are so covered in pigeons, they don't even know which ones got away and tried to land on yours."

"So what you're saying is that the commitment to your bridge is most important."

"Not exactly," I said. "All bridges are temporary. No matter how good they are, exposure to the elements means that they have a fixed lifespan. I just think it's important to conduct proper bridge maintenance for the life of that bridge, so that on any given day, it's a pleasant bridge to travel on. Because you want to make it a pleasant travel experience for you, then proper bridge maintenance isn't a commitment to your bridge, it's a commitment to yourself, about the types of experiences you want to have in your own life."

Jon frowned. "It sounds like you're saying that commitment doesn't really have anything to do with the other person."

I shrugged. "It doesn't," I said. "Sure, it can

affect another person, but you're not really committing to them, and if you think you are, then you're being an idiot. Commitment is the state of being fully present."

Jon shook his head. "You're going to have to explain that one."

"Okay, look. You know how in *The Matrix*, Neo gets the same information downloaded into his head as everyone else."

"Yes."

"Well, remember when Laurence Fishburne could jump a super-long distance and Neo couldn't?"

"Sure."

"Alright, then. Would it have mattered if Neo would have said, 'I promise to super-jump with you until death do us part'? His promises to their super-jumping activities are meaningless because they don't actually impact the outcome. Whether people know it or not, it's not promises and vows to another person that are the important component of commitment, it's the commitment to oneself. Neo had a state of wishy-washiness, and that state of being meant that he couldn't complete the super-jump, even though he told Laurence Fishburne that he was willing to make the leap."

"I think you're missing something," said Jon, which made me raise my eyebrows. He continued: "Yes, you have to commit to yourself, but it's not completely disconnected from the other person. In a relationship commitment, you're entering into an agreement. How you see it is important, but there's another variable in the equation."

"Hmm," I pondered. "Go on."

"Well," he said, "commitment is not just one point. It's not just one thing. I think what you say is true. It starts with the self, but relationships are built on the states of being of both individuals. I think you emphasize the individual, Dr. Matt, partly because you don't like the idea of a relationship changing who you are, because you really like who you are."

"Of course," I said. "Who, if they were me, would not feel the same?"

"It's a fair point," said Jon, smiling. "But commitment isn't being committed to a single point in time, or a single state of space."

"Right," I said. "Commitment happens in the fourth dimension."

"If you mean it is related to time, then that's

right. In a way, it's almost the rejection of being committed to a fixed state. Because everything changes over time, then by being committed to time, you're accepting the state of change. And in a relationship, commitment means that you are coming to terms with the truth of the present, that the relationship is destined to not be the same tomorrow as it is today."

I rubbed my mustache. "I'm still not sure what exactly to do about Midgie."

Jon shrugged. "I'm sure she doesn't know what to do either," he said. "You know, the two of you aren't as different as you think you are."

"What do you mean?"

"Both of you think you are indestructible," he said. "Midgie thinks she is because she is open to *doing* anything in a relationship, and you think you are because you believe you are open to *accepting* anything in a relationship—that you're a go-with-the-flow kinda guy. And because of that, you think you're not affected by normal relationship drama. But, you both got your boundaries pushed on. Midgie did because she doesn't like being told what she can do, and you did because you don't like being told what you should accept. And the reason why it bugged the hell out of you enough to jump back a few steps is because of where you've been hurt."

"You think Midgie and I are alike?" I said.

"You're different and alike," said Jon, "but you both like to focus on where you're different because you're proud of your individuality. But, look at it, Dr. Matt. You both react to getting hurt in the same way, which is the inclination to run away."

"Hmm," I said. "I don't know if I would agree with that. I think I tend to face problems head-on."

Jon cocked his head. "Really? Why did you leave Texas?"

Just then, I got a call on my cell phone. I looked down to see who it was and, strangely enough, it was Midgie calling. I didn't feel it was the right time to answer, so I let it go through to voice mail.

"Was that Midgie?" asked Jon, after I put the phone down.

"Sure was."

"You have a talent for figuring out what to do, Dr. Matt. I wouldn't be too worried about it," Jon said.

"I do have that talent," I said, nodding. "But this thing has me strangely befuddled. It's hard to imagine that with all I know about relationships, I could have overlooked something."

Jon smiled. "You know, for some reason, this reminds me of one of the first houses I built."

"Oh yeah?" I said, taking another sip of the world's greatest soy latte.

He nodded. "It was a big house. We'd finished with all the framing, dry-walling, electrical, even painting and molding for most of the place. One day, I walked into one room, and it just didn't feel right. It felt a lot smaller than I'd anticipated. Sure enough, I went to the blueprints, and it was the wrong dimensions. I even had custom furniture that was already made to go into that room, only now it wasn't going to fit."

"How did that happen?"

"No one wanted to admit a mistake, and insisted they'd done it correctly. When I went through the blueprints everyone had, I found the answer."

"They didn't all match," I said.

"Yep," he said. "Actually, I was the only person with different blueprints, from an earlier design. It's the sort of thing that you would think is absolutely impossible, but it happened."

"That's funny," I said. "So, what did you do?"

"What do you think I did?" said Jon. "I tore that room down and built it over again."

"Huh," I said. "Which house was that?"

"It was my house," Jon said, smiling.

"What room was it?" I asked, trying to picture the many rooms in Jon's house.

Jon chuckled. "I've re-built that house so many times, it doesn't exist anymore."

After leaving the cafe, I called Midgie back. After some chit-chat, she asked if I wanted to meet at Stanley Park in Vancouver for a walk. I thought a walk would do me good, and Midgie is always easy on the eyes, so I said yes.

We met up and I surprised myself by giving that girl a big hug. It's not often that I surprise myself, so the fact that I surprised myself in this way was pretty surprising. I can't say I minded much the big hug I got in return.

We set out on our walk, and, for a while, we just walked and enjoyed the park and didn't say a lot. I know you're probably surprised that there was a period of time that I wasn't talking my mouth off, but some of the things JSR had said had got me thinking.

As we left the park and walked towards the city, Midgie, who knows me well, finally asked what I was thinking about.

"Well, Midgie," I said, "I was thinking that it's about time for our yearly check-in."

"Ah," she said.

"I think it's important to really ask honestly whether or not this is working for us, and if it's something we continue to want in our lives," I said.

"Yes," she said.

"I feel like neither of us would begrudge the other if we decided that some other path was the right way to go, and while, even if this brought us good experiences, there might be something better out there," I said.

"Of course," she said.

"I've learned a lot about relationships over the years by listening to people who have every kind of relationship under the sun."

She listened, quietly.

"My reaction to the news about Kate wasn't so much about you as about Kate," I said. "The thing is, the problem is, well, not a problem but just one of those things... The situation is... I'm still a bit in love with Kate."

Midgie let out a relieved sigh. "And wouldn't you know it, you big mustached man, that Kate is still in love with you?"

"Oh?" I said.

Midgie nodded. "She was distraught that she had hurt you, more than she was that she might hurt me by discontinuing what we had started."

"Oh," I said. "Well, now, this is awkward. But, I didn't come here to talk about Kate. Not yet, anyway."

"I respect that," said Midgie, "but I just want to say that I'm sorry. I didn't mean to hurt you either. That's the last thing I would want to do."

"I know," I said, "and we could both apologize all day long, but that just seems silly. I think we could make a lot of the conversation about what happened, but I'm not sure that what happened has anything to do with what happened."

"I don't think I follow you," said Midgie.

"Well, I just mean that it's possible that there can be bridges so old and so buried in pigeon poop, that you don't even know that there's still a bridge there. I don't know if that's the case or not, but let's not get into what happened just yet."

"So, what *do* you want to talk about?"

"Well, Midgie," I said. "I'm still trying to figure it out. And every time I try to figure it out, it seems like I end up discovering something *else* other than what I'm trying to understand. It is almost enough to make a person feel that, when it comes to you, he's an absolute idiot."

"You're certainly not an idiot," said Midgie, smiling.

"Well, of course not. I said *almost*, but even that feels dangerously close. But the truth is that I don't fully understand you, or this relationship."

"So what do you want to do?" she asked.

"Obviously, there's only one thing *to* do. I've got to take some time and figure it out," I said.

"On your own, you mean?" she asked me.

"Well, no, that's just ridiculous, I can't learn something if it's not in front of me."

She cocked her head. "So, you want to continue our relationship."

"I'm not sure that's going to work either," I said. "Three years of complete bafflement is much too long. I think what I'm going to need is to find out a lot more about you at a much closer distance."

"What do you mean?" she said.

"Well, I'm a little hesitant to say this, but I'm not sure exactly," I said. "What I know is that I've been learning unexpected things from you, and as a person who gives advice, I need to know what else there is to learn. I'd like to think that there's hardly anything else I might gain as knowledge, but history with you seems to indicate otherwise. It's possible that if I want to unravel some of this, I might need to try things I haven't tried before."

"Like what?" she said.

"Again, this is a little embarrassing, but I don't know. Everything in my brain seems to be failing lately, and it's quite disturbing. Fortunately, there's at least a few things I know for sure."

"What's that?" she asked me.

"That I love you, probably about as much as a person can love another human being. And I've missed the heck out of you."

Midgie's eyes did a kind of neat sparkly thing that strangely seems to happen when I simply speak honestly about how I feel. "I think I can relate to that," she said.

"It's kind of a problem," I said.

"A problem?" she asked me.

"I know a lot about relationships," I said, "and I could probably give all the equations and formulas about our relationship and our future, but I may have underestimated a variable, which is love."

"How so?" she asked.

"Love tends to make the predictable unpredictable, and the known unknown. It confounds the chemical reactions, and it alters the physics. That means that whatever goal I aim for, love may mean that I inevitably reach a different destination, because with love, all of reality tends to shift under your feet, like that silly Leonardo DiCaprio movie."

"I see," said Midgie.

"I know you do," I said, "but it means that all I have to go on is right now. And right now, you seem like an absolute necessity in my life. I just can't see it any other way."

Midgie sighed, and seemed to relax in that moment. When I looked at her, I could see that her face was wet with tears, which seemed odd. She's always crying at the strangest times, and I have yet to figure out why.

"But I don't see any point in trying to control the outcome, any more than I would see the point in trying to control who else is in your life," I said.

Midgie looked like she was about to say something, but I kept talking. "You may have been right about a few things," I said. "I'm not saying—" I paused, as something else entered my head.

"Yes?" she said.

"Well," I said. "Pop used to say that the hardest thing to know is when you're wrong, but luckily there are women around to help you."

Midgie laughed. "I wish I could have known him."

"Funny guy," I said. "And he always had a way of saying two things at once. I always thought he was making a joke about nitpicky women, which, as you know, are annoying. But, it's occurred to me just now that maybe he was also being sincere at the same time. I mean, I wouldn't say I was wrong exactly, but somehow you get me to be the best Dr. Matt I can be."

"Thank you."

"You're welcome. But it's even more than that. It's possible that in this relationship, I've felt not just like the best version of myself, but maybe even a new and improved version of myself."

"That's saying something," said Midgie.

"It sure is," I said. "I like who I am, but it's possible that I don't know how much more I might like who I am if I were to stick around."

Midgie smiled. "This has had me thinking, as well. About where we could go in the future—what's *really* possible. I never would have thought we could have come this far."

"Would you like to go further?" I said.

"Well, it turns out that you just spoke the words in my heart, and you spoke them beautifully," she said, beaming at me. "You're right about love making things unpredictable, and love seems to be shifting a few realities already. Not that long ago, I was convinced that you weren't interested in continuing a relationship with me."

"Well, frankly, my dear, you were being an idiot," I said, which brought a laugh from Midgie.

"And," I continued reluctantly, "it's possible, quite possible, that I was being an idiot as well."

Folks, that unexpectedly got me a set of arms around my neck and a giant smooch in the middle of the sidewalk in downtown Vancouver by the sexiest and neatest lady I've ever known.

I took her arm in mine, and we walked up the street, towards something that had caught my eye. Two months earlier, I might have passed it by, or waited for Midgie to say something about it, assuming that it was much more her domain than mine. But, if I was going to figure this girl out, then something might need to change. Or maybe something already had.

"Let me tell you about a time when I was even more of an idiot, which is the reason I left Texas," I said. "But first..." I said, and I stopped on the sidewalk.

"Let's go into this sex shop."

The End

About Dr. Matt

Dr. Matt is a world-famous author and all-around amazing person. If you haven't heard of him, then you may need to start by asking yourself, "Self, what have I been doing with my time? *Why have I even been alive?*"

Then, you're going to want to pick up a phone and call all your friends. "Frank, have you heard of Dr. Matt?" you'll say.

"Of course," your friend Frank will say. "He's The Most Famous Fake Doctor Of Our Time™. Where have you been?"

Then, you'll call Barbara. "Barb, have you ever heard of someone who calls themselves 'The Most Famous Fake Doctor Of Our Time' ?"

"You mean Dr. Matt?" Barbara will say.

"What the bejeezus!" you'll exclaim, and will slam the phone down. Frantically, you'll begin Googling online, getting the sinking feeling that the most amazing phenomenon in the history of mankind has begun and *you nearly missed out.*

Finally, Google will begin to give you hope. Links to podcasts, blogs, books, videos, Facebook pages, and Twitter feeds will begin to appear, with the reassuring mustached image of Dr. Matt. A ray of sunshine will emerge from the clouds and fall upon your face.

You will weep.

Dr. Matt lives in Vancouver, B.C. Do not stalk him, unless it is absolutely necessary.

www.ingramcontent.com/pod-product-compliance
Lightning Source LLC
Chambersburg PA
CBHW020419290526
45785CB00002B/627